Beyond the Craft

Essential Skills for Small Business Success

Published by the Power Writers Publishing Group in 2024.

Peta Stewart copyright 2024.

All Rights Reserved. No part of this book may be reproduced by any mechanical, photographic, or electronic processes, or in the form of a phonographic recording. Nor may it be stored in a retrieval system, transmitted or otherwise copied for public or private use other than for 'fair use' as brief quotations embodied in articles and reviews, without prior written permission of the publisher.

ISBN: 978-1-7635809-0-9

A catalogue record for this work is available from the National Library of Australia

Cover design by Publishious
Internal layout by Publishious

Disclaimer

Any opinions expressed in this work are exclusively those of the author and are not necessarily the views held or endorsed by others quoted throughout. All of the information, exercises and concepts contained within the publication are intended for general information only. The author does not take any responsibility for any choices that any individual or organization may make relating to this information in the business, personal, financial, familial, or other areas of life. If any individual or organization does wish to implement the ideas discussed herein, it is recommended that they obtain their own independent advice specific to their circumstances.

ACKNOWLEDGEMENTS

First and foremost, a huge thank you to my husband, Daz. You once said, "I don't really support you, my love, as you would still do what you do without me." That always makes me chuckle. The support you provide by simply standing by as I pursue my dreams is both remarkable and essential. You never question or second-guess my plans, dreams, or strategies. Your unconditional support means the world to me—lots of love.

When I asked you during the writing of this book whether to call you Daz or Daryl, you replied, "just call me 'silent partner'." Ha! It's another testament to the silent, yet steadfast support you offer, acting like a safety net beneath my endeavours.

To my mentor and friend, Peter Cook, thank you for teaching me what I didn't even know I needed to learn, for being the sounding board I required, and for ensuring I never dream small.

To my book coach, Jane Turner, I am grateful that the universe brought us together. It was incredibly comforting to have you in my corner throughout this process.

To all the clients and team members at Peta Stewart Property Conveyancers, past and present, I have learned and grown immensely thanks to each of you. I am grateful for your contributions to my journey.

Finally, to my mentor clients, thank you for allowing me to be a part of your journeys, which in turn, has brought a new level of fulfillment to my life.

CONTENTS

PREFACE i

INTRODUCTION v

PART ONE – YOU

    CHAPTER ONE: The Matter of Self-Care 1

    CHAPTER TWO: The Importance of Energy 15

    CHAPTER THREE: The Advantage of Emotional Intelligence .. 26

PART TWO – TEAM

    CHAPTER FOUR: The Value of Support 35

    CHAPTER FIVE: The Power of Relationships 50

    CHAPTER SIX: The Challenge of Leadership 58

PART THREE – WORLD

    CHAPTER SEVEN: The Magic of Service 77

    CHAPTER EIGHT: The Art of Social Media 83

    CHAPTER NINE: The Gift of Competition 91

CONCLUSION 97

ABOUT THE AUTHOR 99

PREFACE

When I first got the idea to write a book, I felt like I wanted to use it to promote the benefits of running a business in 'the bush' (as we call anywhere outside of the cities in Australia where I'm based). I'm a real advocate for life in the bush because of the way I feel when I get home after speaking at conferences or delivering training programs for organisations located in Sydney and Melbourne which are the two biggest cities in Australia.

Don't get me wrong, they are both beautiful places with a lot going for them, but from where I sit, life in the country is the only way to go for me. I couldn't ever see myself giving up the slower pace of life in the country, or the proximity to nature, and space in general. Then there's the disincentive of the relative stress of commuting in the cities where burgeoning populations have shown up weaknesses in relation to planning and infrastructure.

What's more, I could be wrong, but I don't see much evidence of the sort of community spirit that is fostered and easy to establish in the bush. There's also the question of the cost of living to consider. The way I see it, people who have oodles of money and can afford to live near the beach or overlooking Sydney Harbour have got it made, but if it was a question of living in the suburbs and commuting to and from the city every day, I'd say forget it.

So now that I've got that off my chest, I feel really proud to be able to give something back and pay forward my good fortune of living a life I love and doing work I find really fulfilling by writing this book.

I have the greatest respect for people who are in the business of helping others. Like the staff in my business helping people buying or selling a property, to being a celebrant who marries people and everything in between. This respect stems from the understanding that running a business is a challenging endeavour, fraught with adversity that tests the resilience, adaptability, and strategic thinking of anyone who enters the business world without full awareness of its demands.

That said, even those with their eyes wide open are not immune to the almost inevitable ups and downs that come with the territory. There's not only the financial risk involved, especially for those requiring significant capital to get their business off the ground. There's also the risk to their health and their relationships to be considered as well.

The kind of financial uncertainty I'm referring to here is compounded by fluctuating market conditions, competition, and changing consumer demands. If Covid taught us anything, it's that people like us need to be prepared to continuously innovate and adapt to stay relevant and profitable. That alone can be a daunting and financially draining process.

Moreover, running a business involves managing operational challenges including hiring and retaining skilled employees, maintaining a healthy workplace culture, and ensuring efficient workflow processes are in place. In other words, entrepreneurs often find themselves wearing multiple hats, and juggling roles ranging from marketing and sales to human resources, with customer service thrown in for good measure. This can lead to overwhelm and burnout, especially in small businesses where resources are limited. Additionally, regulatory compliance adds another layer of complexity, as businesses are required to adhere to laws and regulations that can vary greatly depending on the location and industry in question.

Despite these challenges, many people find running a business deeply rewarding. I have written this book for anyone starting out in business, and those who already have a business but are struggling to feel rewarded because they're finding it hard to keep their head above water. Essentially, this book is about helping those people to avoid some of the pitfalls I fell into back in the day. Burnout serves as a prime example.

I've read numerous business books myself, and I've learned that the best way to truly benefit from the time we spend reading is to reflect on how the information within those pages applies to our own lives. The only problem is that it's easy to forget to do that. But fear not, I've got you covered. At the end of each chapter, I've included reflective questions for you to consider, unpack, and determine where you can take action.

I want to commend you for reading this book, and I want to wish you all the very best for a future that involves running a fulfilling and profitable business.

INTRODUCTION

It's likely you will have at least one thing in common with me. If being a savvy businessperson had nothing to do with your decision to start your business, then you're one of those people. If you're anything like I was, you opened your business because you are excellent at your craft. And you figured the clients who were coming into the business being run by your boss would be much better served if you had the freedom to do things the way you do them best. That was certainly the case for me.

Essentially, I was (and still am) an expert when it comes to property conveyancing, and after working in the space since 1999, it made a lot of sense to open my own conveyancing business. The rest is history because that's exactly what I did. When I first started out, I loved having the autonomy to do things the way I wanted to, and to serve clients in a way that was fulfilling both for them and for me. The only problem was that there is more to running a business than being a well-qualified expert of one kind or other.

It really doesn't make any difference if we've gone to the best university and completed a degree, or finished an apprenticeship with flying colours, or received extensive on the job training to master the technical skills required in our industry. I say that because if we lack the critical business skills to keep the doors open and food on the table, then unless we're lucky enough to tap into divine intervention of some kind, or funding is available to bring a business manager onboard, odds are that the business is going to falter.

Doing the conveyancing work when I opened my business was the easy part. The challenging part was dealing with the unseen complexity of things like hiring competent staff, creating a healthy culture, and handling responsibilities around accounting, marketing, leadership, and human resource management. These are just a few of the hats we need to be comfortable wearing to run a successful small business.

Opening my business was an 'interesting' time for me to say the least, because (among other things) I wasn't aware of the intricacies inherent in wearing the hats I just mentioned. The first challenge I had to come to terms with was the fact that I was exceptionally good and exceptionally average at the same time. I wasn't used to that dichotomy being in place, and I didn't like it one little bit.

If you ask most micro to medium business owners why they opened their business, I'm prepared to bet you won't hear many of them saying "because I am good at running a business". The answer is more likely to be "because I wanted to build houses my way", or "I was sick of working for someone else", or "I wanted to spread my unique process for brewing coffee to a worldwide audience", or something like that.

I'm imagining what motivated you to pick this book up as I'm writing this introduction. You might or might not resonate with what I'm about to say, but what I know is that I wrote this book for the business owner who is kick-ass at their craft, but missing out on opportunities to be successful and have that beautiful thing called peace of mind when their head hits the pillow at the end of the day.

I know what it's like to be running a business on gut instinct, wondering what all the noise about the importance of things like culture and leadership is all about. In fact, the decisions I made around what to include and what to leave out of this book were based on my experience of being in that position when I opened my own business. So, what you will find in the chapters to come are bite sized pieces of information that you can easily action to improve your results.

INTRODUCTION

I'm not trying to cover all of the bases here. I'm giving you practical hands-on advice based on what has worked well for me. I've written this book because I wanted to share what I've learnt over the years of running my business so that you won't need to waste the amount of energy that I did to get to where I am now. The thing is that I love imagining you having more time to focus on what you are really good at because you've had a heads up about what's involved in running a successful business through reading this book.

I smile when I remember the feelings that came up when I first started to think about writing a book. Basically, I had no idea where to start. In fact, two years passed before I actually started to nut out my content. The only reason it didn't blow out to four years or more is that I engaged a writing coach to work with me. I don't know why I didn't do it sooner, because if I've learnt one thing in business, it's to surround yourself with people to support you in the areas you are not so good at. And in case you're wondering, the irony of me not knowing where to start a book that's about helping people who don't know where to start when it comes to setting up a business with solid foundations in place, was not lost on me.

It's a no-brainer really when you think about it. There's no point in beating ourselves up about not knowing what we don't know. What you probably do know that is relevant here is that things should be easier and a whole lot less stressful than they often are. So this book is about filling you in on the things that will set you up with the kinds of foundations that will position you to succeed without losing your passion for what you do in the process.

What this book is not about is justifying my decision to avoid moving from the bush to the city in the belief that the city is where successful businesses need to be. I say that because I had a little bit of a chip on my shoulder that I wasn't entirely conscious of when I decided it was time for me to document everything I know for those coming behind me. In fact, I even had a subheading with the words 'Why business in the bush?' in mind.

Let me explain where I'm coming from by way of sharing a bit of my background with you. I always had the sense of being subordinate to my fellow students who were from the big smoke when I was studying Conveyancing Law and Practice at Macquarie University campus which is located in Sydney. The problem was that at least a part of me equated the fact that the city was dynamic, fast paced, forward thinking, and trendy to mean that rural areas and towns were not. Sure enough, there are many more job opportunities in the city, but after shaking the monkey off my back years ago and running a successful business in the country since 2009, it's obvious that while there are advantages to being based in the city, there are also advantages to running a business outside of the metropolitan centers as well.

I'm prepared to cut my younger self some slack here because I used to be an elite track cyclist. In that context, it was definitely harder to get access to the opportunities and facilities that my contemporaries who lived in the city took for granted. For example, I didn't have the kind of ease of access to the indoor tracks that the local cyclists had. That meant I had to factor in extra time to travel to venues for competitions and training. In fact, just about everything was harder for a track cyclist like me who lived 300 kilometres north-east of Melbourne and 580 kilometres south-west of Sydney. Among other things, more travel meant less recovery time and less time to train. It was a real battle for me. In a sense I was torn between the sport I loved and the place I loved living in.

Fast forward 20 years, and I can say without hesitation that I believe my business would not have been as successful as it is if it was in the city. It's not just that my conveyancing business is absolutely thriving in the country environment. It's also being reminded every so often to thank my lucky stars for the way things have turned out

INTRODUCTION

whenever I find myself having to deal with the logistical challenges in the city. These include the time spent stuck in traffic, having to navigate my way around crowds, and queuing for ages to get a takeaway chai latte. There's also the extra time it takes to get from my hotel to the venue of the conference I'm speaking at, or the office of one of my corporate clients who brought me in to provide training for their staff.

In the end, my cycling career didn't survive the downside of the time involved in commuting from my home in Albury to the city and back again many times over. Although I had some successes along the way, my results didn't match my dreams or the level of my talent. That said, every cloud has a silver lining (as they say), and the skills I learnt as an elite athlete on the cycling circuit filtered into my business. This was particularly the case in relation to creating a high performing culture within my company.

I know there are plenty of people out there who are like I was during the early years of being my own boss, but don't worry if you're not one of them. There will still be plenty of tips around building your business that you'll take away from reading this book. Not least of which is the reflections you'll be reminded to document at the end of each chapter. To be honest, I feel like this is actually where the real gold is waiting to be mined.

I'm going to finish this introduction by telling you a little bit more about myself. I'm doing this because I appreciate the fact that you're running a busy business, and you don't have a whole lot of spare time to read a book that's been written by someone you've never even heard of. So you might like to know that I was 29 when I opened my own conveyancing business. I was young, eager, ambitious, and incredibly naive. I was also blind to the fact that the technical skills and knowledge needed to be an excellent conveyancer are very different to the tools needed to build a sustainable and successful conveyancing business.

Needless to say, I could have definitely used a book like this myself back then. I say that because I'm sharing the kinds of insights and tools they don't teach you at university. Sure, there are business courses people like us can take, but the kind of business tips, tricks and hacks that you'll find in the chapters that follow have come from the lessons I've learnt through the day-to-day grind of the startup phase and beyond.

On a practical level, when I started my business in 2009, I rented a room and bought some secondhand furniture from a clearance sale. Even with these humble beginnings, I did very well in my first year with revenue close to $100,000.00 coming through the door. More than a decade later, I'm running a very successful 7-figure conveyancing business that provides conveyancers with development programs and support to maximise their results. One of the keys to the success of my business is that our clients are treated like rock stars. As a result of that, they are our cheerleaders who talk us up whenever the opportunity arises.

And me – well I am still learning every day. An environment where continual learning is the norm is another one of the keys to the success I've experienced in my business.

To really get down to my core intention now, I want you to know that I've written this book with the goal of shortcutting your journey to running a profitable business that doesn't pave the way to an early grave. That might sound like a harsh thing to say, but sadly, I've seen way too many businesspeople working way too hard for way too long to the detriment of important things like good quality sleep and spending time with loved ones.

My hope is that you will be able to leapfrog over some of the kinds of mistakes I made to get to where I am now. In other words, I want to fast track your journey to business success. You

INTRODUCTION

will of course make your own mistakes along the way. That's not such a bad thing though, because one of the quickest ways to learn something is to find out what doesn't work. That's what personal development and growth looks like. That said, if you use this book wisely and don't fall into the trap of skipping over the reflection opportunities at the end of each chapter, you will position yourself to be able to cherry pick your way through the approaches I have used in the course of taking my business to seven figures.

I've had people ask me why I would want to share my secrets around success with my potential competitors. The answer is that I love the conveyancing industry. And the way I see it, the more knowledge there is in the industry, the better the standard of service will be. Furthermore, leaving a legacy like this that ultimately benefits the society we are a part of results in everyone winning.

There's a quote that I read once that has stuck with me because it shines a light on the fact that I've found my true north in the worlds of business and mentoring, as well as conveyancing. The quote is:

> *Success isn't just about what you accomplish in your life.
> It's about what you inspire others to do.*
> Unknown

In other words, having a successful business is not enough for me. Building and sharing something that can inspire others to succeed is what gets me up in the morning and gives me a deep sense of purpose.

Finally, before we dive into the content of the book, I want to share the Beyond the Craft model that structures how I think about business, and the way the book itself is structured.

	You	Team	World
Evolution	Emotional Intelligence	Leadership	Competition
Entrepreneurial	Energy	Relationships	Social-Media
Foundation	Self-care	Support	Service

As you can see in the model above, running a successful business is about how **you** turn up, the quality of your **team**, and the impact you have on the **world** (whether you're aware of it or not). The model is layered from a foundational level, developing to an entrepreneurial level and an evolutionary level we should all aspire to be.

The first part of the book is about you. It relates to self-care at the foundational level, followed by the energy you emanate, and finally the level of your emotional intelligence. It's true what they say - 'It all starts with you'. By starting this journey focusing on your wellbeing, you set a strong groundwork for resilience and vitality. Often, business owners put their own needs last, prioritising the demands of the business above all else. This section teaches you about the pitfalls of neglecting self-care and how such oversight can sneak up on you, potentially leading to burnout and detrimentally affecting the health of both the entrepreneur and the business.

Part Two is about the team. It's about who you've got on your bus supporting you. This is where you get to consider how well you rate yourself in terms of your leadership through looking at the quality of the relationships you nurture, and the results of your team.

And the last section is about how your business is positioned in the bigger picture of the world around you. We approach this question from the point of view of the quality of the service you provide, the way you position your business within the market, and how you differentiate it from your competitors. This is about attracting and retaining the right clients, and having the confidence to run your own race without worrying about what others in your industry are doing.

Now that you've got a better handle on what I'm all about, I want to invite you to read on and avoid being a passive observer. The best way to do that is to not skip over the reflection pages.

PART ONE:
You

CHAPTER ONE:
The Matter of Self-Care

Energy is your currency.

Knowing what burnout is like from firsthand experience, I take the matter of self-care very seriously. Depending on where you sit on the spectrum from being a frantic workaholic to a complete slacker, you will either benefit greatly from unpicking the question of what self-care actually looks like, or decide to skip over this chapter.

I guess there's a third category of people I should acknowledge. They are the people who also take self-care seriously like I do, and already have a strategy in place to keep themselves well. They could be forgiven for skipping over this chapter, but chances are they won't. I say that because they're likely to be on the lookout for new ideas and products or services that emerge around self-care.

Self-care is a broad concept that encompasses various practices, habits, and attitudes aimed at maintaining our overall wellbeing. It's an integral part of living a balanced and healthy life, both mentally and physically. Here are some of the fundamental aspects of self-care:

1. **Physical health**: This is often what people first think of when the matter of self-care is raised. It includes activities that maintain the body's health and functioning, such as regular exercise, getting adequate sleep, healthy eating, and preventive healthcare. The great thing is that exercise doesn't just keep the body fit. It also releases endorphins, which are known as

the feel-good hormones that we all love. Adequate sleep is crucial for mental and physical recovery, while a balanced diet provides the necessary nutrients for bodily functions.

2. **Mental and emotional health**: Mental and emotional self-care involves practices that help us to manage stress, anxiety, and other emotional states. This can include mindfulness practices such as meditation, engaging in hobbies or activities that we enjoy, and seeking professional help like therapy or counselling when necessary. In addition, simple things like journaling can be a powerful tool for processing emotions and fostering self-awareness.

3. **Social connection**: Having a supportive social network is vital for emotional resilience. Self-care in this context involves maintaining nurturing relationships with friends and family, participating in community activities, or simply engaging in meaningful conversations. It's important to balance social interactions with personal time, as both are essential for emotional wellbeing.

4. **Personal growth and self-compassion**: Self-compassion involves setting realistic goals, engaging in continuous learning, and being kind to ourselves. It's essential to recognise that self-care is not about striving for perfection, but about making continuous, small improvements and understanding that it's okay to have setbacks.

5. **Spiritual wellbeing**: For many, spiritual or religious practices form a crucial part of self-care. This could involve meditation, prayer, attending religious services, or spending time in nature. These practices can provide a sense of purpose, connection, and inner peace.

Meditation:

This brings me to the question of the benefits of meditation. I'm just going to say it like it is. Having a daily meditation practice fast tracked my journey to running a successful business that doesn't run me into the ground.

I've never been a religious person, and things like meditation seemed a bit too far down the 'woo woo' scale for me not so long ago. However, in the case of almost every podcast I listened to, or book I read about successful high performers, I was hearing people say that their success comes down in no small part to meditating regularly and frequently. And one day the thought "who do I think I am being so arrogant to think that somehow I'm above benefiting from something like meditation."

That's when it dawned on me that if I wanted to play at the level of the high performers whose books I read and podcasts I listen to, then I'd need to incorporate the same kinds of habits they live by. And since I live nowhere near the beach to take early morning cold water dunks (which also seems to be a popular strategy high performers use) – then meditation it was.

Luckily my business mentor and friend Peter Cook is an Ishaya Monk. He also teaches the Ishaya's Ascension which is a form of meditation. So, I guess it was meant to be, and rather than wading through the huge range of options to learn how to meditate, I started learning the Ishaya approach in 2022.

Yes - you do have to learn to meditate. It doesn't just fall into place. I smile when I think about the number of people who have said things to me like – "oh I tried meditation once, but I couldn't get into it", or "my mind wouldn't be quiet, so I got up and did something else", or even, "who has time for that". I know those kinds of excuses only too well. In my own case, the fact that I managed to establish a routine around meditation came down to hanging in there until the results started showing up. My motivation to keep going was a given when that happened.

It all started with a three-day meditation course. That gave me the tools I needed to commit to giving it a go for 20 minutes per day for six months. My intention was to check in with myself at the six month point and decide whether it was worth continuing. In the beginning, the thought of 20 minutes per day actually heightened my anxiety to be honest. The voice in my head was saying "Who has a spare 20 minutes floating around?" Well apparently, people like Bill Gates, Ray Dalio and Oprah Winfrey do. So I figured if they could find time for daily meditation, then so should I. What's more, knowing Pete as well as I do it was easy to choose his meditation method without needing to research which approach would be best for me.

I told my team at work about the commitment I'd made to myself. And because of the relationship I'd built with them, they were fully onboard. They weren't only respectful in relation to quarantining me from interruptions during my meditation time, but also by helping me to stay accountable. That made a huge difference. As did the fact that Pete was there to help me stay accountable as well.

At the start Pete would ask me how my daily practice was going. I'm proud to say that after a month he didn't need to ask me anymore. Even though I might miss a day here or there, rather than letting that derail me, it motivated me to do whatever I needed to do to embed meditation into my life. Coming up to the six month point I wasn't sure if there were any results in the sense that it didn't feel like anything had changed.

But then something important happened, my work team started telling me they were noticing some very positive changes in me. These included things like my moods being less erratic, and me being a lot less stressed and calmer overall. I knew the changes must have been significant because this feedback was coming from my staff without me asking for it. That feedback, coupled with the fact that the flow-on effect of my meditation practice contributed to the wellbeing of my staff, provided enough of an incentive for me to keep going.

It's worth noting that my main motivation for continuing to meditate stems from the responsibility I feel when it comes to creating a positive work environment for my staff. Meditation took on a deeper significance when it extended beyond just my own personal success and wellbeing. I shifted my focus from merely enhancing my performance to using meditation as a tool to be the best wife, leader, mentor, step-mum, and friend possible.

When I shifted the focus in that way, there was no way I was going to let those special people in my life down. From my own point of view, when I was still quite new to meditation, a couple of the key benefits of my practice where that it mitigated my anxiety, and it made me incredibly calm under pressure. Among other things, being able to take everything in my stride made me a whole lot more effective and efficient. The fact is that by the six-month point, my regular practice had seriously boosted my productivity in general and my brainpower in particular.

It was a great case of slowing down to speed up. If I ever started to feel like I was becoming frantic, rushed, or overwhelmed, I could just stop and meditate. That inevitably got me back on an even footing so that I could turn up at work and home and be fully present. Sure, things could still flare up from time to time, but they didn't chew up my energy and position me to be a prime candidate for an ulcer like they used to.

One unexpected and quite beautiful biproduct of my meditation practice was that a natural kind of self-love started to rear its head. So much so that I was shocked to realise how low it had been to start off with. This generated a whole lot of interesting results. For example, I started spending less money on meaningless things. Those 'add to cart' endorphin hits just weren't needed as much as they used to be anymore. I also got to know myself a whole lot better. A good example is that before I had the benefit of meditation under my belt, I wasn't even remotely aware that I was a bit of an 'add to cart' junkie.

That's what lead to me progressing to a point where I became spiritual. When I say that, I want to be clear that what I'm talking about has nothing to do with being religious. It's about extending my focus beyond the physical realm and believing there is something within me that is greater than myself. This level of awareness was an unexpected result that I credit with the very unexpected boost in the success of my business.

Those who knew me prior to my daily meditation practice really kicking in would never have expected me to become a spiritual person. What's more, anyone who spends every minute of every day in the logical part of their head could never even start to understand how being spiritual could help when it comes to running a successful business.

I never try to convince people to see the world the way I do, but I figure that as you're still reading this chapter, you might be interested in how spirituality could have a positive impact on your business. So here are the things that came up when I thought about that:

1. **Reframing failure:** Spiritual perspectives allow for the belief that personal growth and learning comes out of every experience we have, even if they are not positive ones. I don't view failure as a devastating end, but as a step in the learning process and an opportunity for growth. Among other things, this reduces the fear associated with taking risks. I will often tell myself "the Universe has my back" or ask, "what is the Universe trying to teach me here?"
2. **Gaining more inner peace and confidence:** As I go about my business in a state of being centred and calm, I can approach any business risks I'm facing with a clearer mind and more confidence. I believe that result comes from

knowing that my self-worth is not solely tied to the successes or failures I experience in my business.
3. **Being able to trust the journey:** Spirituality often involves trusting the journey of life and believing that there is a larger plan or order to the things that happen on a daily basis. This kind of trust can alleviate the pressure of needing to control every outcome, and allow for a more comfortable relationship with uncertainty and risk.
4. **Gaining detachment from outcomes:** By focusing on effort and intention rather than on results, I can take risks without being paralysed by the fear of what might happen if things don't go as planned.
5. **Increasing intuition:** I believe my meditation practice has heightened my intuition, which is a powerful tool to have in business and in life. These days I always listen and trust that inner voice that comes up from time to time.

I went to New Zealand for a weeklong meditation retreat with the Ishaya monks six months after I started to practice meditation. Hands down, this was the best investment in personal development I have ever made. The connection with myself and my mind that I first experienced at the retreat has made a big difference to the way my life is playing out. The ability to be present enabled me to say goodbye to being anxious about the future, as well as questioning the past. Things like clarity, calmness and focus are now the order of the day for me.

In summary, my daily meditation practice has proved to be a great asset in relation to my business. These days, my minimum is 20 minutes per day and on a good day I will get up to three x 20 minute meditations in. Because of this, my mental health has never been better, and I have never been more productive. Another outcome that is very important to me is the ability to be entirely present with the people I interact with. I can do that because I've developed the ability to block out all the other 'noise' are lives can be filled with.

Here is a list of the benefits my meditation practice as brought me.

- Stress reduction
- Improved concentration and focus
- Enhanced Emotional Intelligence
- Better decision making
- Increased creativity
- Improved communication skills
- Greater resilience
- Enhanced leadership qualities
- Health benefits
- Improved time management
- Reduced anxiety
- Increased patience.

When you look at that list, I bet you'd pay good money for a pill that provided all that wouldn't you? Me too! So, Peta the non-believer became a believer, and if it feels right, I'd encourage you to find something that achieves those kinds of results as well.

Work/Life Balance:
I've been known to say that work/life balance is BS. The way I see it, work/life balance is an anxiety inducing mythical form of perfectionism that does more harm than good. Before I explain what I believe the solution to the elusive question of work/life balance is, I want you to know that I am able to be dispassionate when it comes to this topic. I say that because I have expertise on both sides of the equation having been to the very extremes of burnout myself.

Not unlike many new business owners motivated to do well, I poured everything I had into the business when I first started out. In fact, I didn't take a holiday for six years, and I slept in my office more times than I can believe now. To compound the physical toll on my body, I also started eating poorly and exercising less.

I was obsessing over the work details and fixating on perfection in relation to everything. If I was awake, I would be working, or thinking about work.

I wouldn't recommend that approach to anyone. In my case, the consequences of 80 hour working weeks included a divorce, stuffed up hormones, needing a stomach operation, living with high functioning anxiety, undergoing two sinus operations, and the legacy of several strained relationships with friends and family members. But do you know what another consequence of living my life in a way that was leading me toward an early death was? It was having a successful business. That's why overworking to achieve success can be so alluring.

Among other things, this begs the question of the definition of success. Common definitions describe success as the accomplishment of an aim or purpose. That's all very well and good, but it doesn't do a lot to help us articulate what success looks like to us. That's because by its very nature success is totally subjective. What this means is that all you need to worry about is achieving what success looks like to you.

Over time, I've learnt that for me success is not just about the tangible things like profit and loss, client numbers, and market share. For me, success also includes achieving a sense of fulfillment, and providing a high level of customer satisfaction. It also includes delivering impactful leadership, developing and maintaining a high performing culture, and making positive connections.

If you're like some of the people I share this information with, you might be wondering how I wound up making more money while working less. The answer is because I choose projects that matter and lean right in. Let me dissect this idea for you. My mentor and great friend Peter Cook who you've heard a lot about already, hit the nail on the head in his book called *The New Rules of Management*. In it he wrote - "I don't think the key to being successful in your business or career, your relationships, your health, your finances or anything else for that matter is being well resourced or intelligent, or even well connected – although these things all help. I think the single most important factor in your success is your ability to implement significant projects."

For me work/life balance has nothing to do with an equal balance between work and rest/play. It has nothing to do with how many hours here and how many hours there. And I truly believe working a perfect amount of hours each week (whatever that number is) is for those with tepid motivation and ambition. When I am working on a project that matters, I lean in hard. That means I will still pull a 60 hour week when a project needs me to. And I do that willingly without resentment or regret of any kind. In fact, I enjoy it because I love the thrill of accomplishment, and revel in the face of success in relation to doing work that matters.

So you might be wondering how I manage that kind of 'leaning in' without the burnout and consequences I experienced in the past. Well, it all comes down to awareness. The difference now is that I have awareness around my state. That means I know when I need to lean back out. And when I lean back into my personal life, I lean in hard. That way I make sure that I fill my cup the way I need to stay well.

It's less a question of a balance and more like a see-saw. Just before your bum hits the ground on one side of the see saw, it's time to bounce back up and let the other side of your life have your time and attention. I also communicate with those around me more regularly and effectively. For example, I always let my family know when I am about to go deep into a project that means I may not be around as much as usual for a while. A consequence of that is that I am able to be completely present with them at the end of the project. That way I get their buy-in because they know that while I'm going to be head down and bum up for a while, sometime soon I will be completely present with them.

What I'd recommend if you're struggling to cope or feeling like you're at risk of going down the track that leads to burnout, in addition to getting help from a professional if you feel like you need to, is to:

1. Define what success looks like for you, not only in relation to your career or business, but also in relation to your family, health, and possibly giving back in some way.
2. Consider how you could create triggers that will alert you when you're at risk of leaning into your business too hard.
3. Start advising key family members when you need to work on something important so that they know it's not a great time to heap additional pressure on you.

I was having an infrared sauna in the middle of writing this chapter when an affirmation card with the words "The true measure of success is a calm nervous system" was given to me by the wellness studio. I thought it was interesting that I was writing about the definition of success on the same day as that card was given to me. This got me thinking that if we all had clarity around our own definition of success, fulfilling that definition would result in all of us having a calm nervous system. That conclusion is based on the fact that we would be less stressed because we were living the life we've designed for ourselves. This approach doesn't require having a magic number of hours balanced between life and business. I say that because it's about only taking on projects that matter, and having the awareness to lean back into the personal side of our life when required.

For me, these days when I have times where I am leaning hard into work, I also now make a conscious effort to be completely present in the personal moments. So, when I am not working, I am not thinking about work, and I ensure the time I spend with loved ones is not filtered through a wandering work-focused mind. I honestly believe there is no magical ratio that determines the way we should apportion our energy between work and life. The way I see it, to be successful and fulfilled we need to lean in when it is needed, and then know when to lean back out again.

The real strength is having the awareness of knowing when it's time to lean into business and when it's time to lean into life. If I have a big work project on, I am going to lean full tilt into the business and get it done. This is not negotiable because the old cliché that hard work pays off is right. At the same time, we need to know when it's time to lean more into life in order to enjoy sustained success and happiness.

These days, I regularly plan chunks of time to go away on meditation and/or health retreats where I don't even take my computer or phone with me. This is what I mean when I say that I lean as far as possible away from work as I can. I also make sure I switch my brain completely off. This is how I choose to navigate the matter of sharing my time and energy between business and life. The bottom line is that you will have far more success by going all in, then leaning back out, rather than just cruising along doing a mediocre job of running your business and living your life.

Burnout:
As I said earlier, I know what burnout is like, and I never want to go there again. In fact, if you take nothing else away from reading this book but an appreciation of the things you can do to avoid burnout, I will be a happy woman.

So what is burnout? It's a state of emotional, physical, and mental exhaustion caused by excessive and prolonged stress (often related to work). People in a state of burnout are likely to feel overwhelmed, emotionally drained, and unable to meet the constant demands life puts on them. As the stress continues, people with burnout tend to lose interest in things. Needless to say, it reduces productivity and saps our energy, leaving us feeling increasingly helpless, hopeless, and potentially resentful because we've arrived at a place where we feel like we have nothing more to give.

The problem is that the negative effects of burnout spill over into every area of life. It can also cause long-term changes to our body that make us vulnerable to illnesses of all kinds. This is because our nervous system takes an absolute beating as a result of the chronic stress associated with burnout. This can also disrupt the balance of neurotransmitters in the brain such as dopamine and norepinephrine. That's the last thing we want because these neurotransmitters are responsible for regulating our moods in particular, and our mental wellbeing overall.

If that's not reason enough for you to take self-care (especially in relation to your stress levels) seriously, you should also consider the fact that some of the other symptoms of burnout include an escalation in self-doubt and/or a sense of failure, as well as feeling helpless, trapped, and/or defeated. Then there's the loss of motivation to take into account as well.

The bottom line in relation to recovering from burnout or avoiding it altogether, is that strategies around things like changes in lifestyle, tapping into support from loved ones, and seeking professional help can be crucial. If you fall victim to burnout like I did, the upside to making it out the other side is that you will have amassed the tools that enabled you to get back to a state of wellbeing and equilibrium. What's more, these tools are the ones that will be crucial to avoiding burnout if it ever rears its head again.

In essence, self-care is simply about being mindful of our needs and taking steps to meet them. It is not a one-size-fits-all scenario, but rather a personal matter that varies from person to person. Before I sign off on this chapter, I want to stress that it's important to accept that self-care is not selfish. In fact, it's a necessary and fundamental aspect of living a healthy, fulfilling life.

YOUR REFLECTIONS

- What self-care activity can you commit to daily for improved wellbeing?
- Recall a time you felt overwhelmed. What's one strategy you could use to avoid that in the future?
- How do you define a successful day in terms of self-care and work accomplishments?
- Of the five fundamental aspects of self-care, which one are you best at? And which is your Achilles heel?
- In moments of high stress, what quick technique helps you regain a sense of calm?

CHAPTER TWO:
The Importance of Energy

Energy is an intangible yet measurable asset that we can deliberately manage, protect, and leverage for personal and professional gain.

Have you ever watched a keynote speaker and found yourself being mesmerized? How about being at the supermarket paying for your groceries sensing that the checkout person would rather be anywhere else than there through the negative vibes they were giving off? Or have you noticed the way the mood lifted when a person walked into a party you were at and lit the room up? How about a peaceful feeling you got from the person on the mat next to you in your yoga class?

These are all examples of the fact that the energy we give off is recognisable. Why I bring this up here is that our energy is amplified in business. What I mean by that is that when we have low energy, the impact it will have on our business could be dire. Whereas when our energy as the leader of the business is positive, we are creating the kind of environment needed to enable the people within it to thrive.

I wasn't conscious of this until I hired staff and noticed that the way I walked into the room had an immediate effect on them. If I bounced in full of positive energy and a big smile, the energy in the office lifted and my staff started giving off positive vibes too. Whereas, if I walked in with stress written all over my face and locked myself in my private office to get through my work, the energy overall would become quite tense and on edge.

So, what I want you to know as the leader of your business is that whether you are aware of it or not, your energy is in the spotlight more than anyone else's. What's more, it can set the tone for the whole team. Likewise, the energy you take into client meetings will influence the outcome.

I used to have an accountant who was bland in every sense of the word. His wardrobe was monotone, there was no modulation in the tone of his voice, he barely made eye contact, and his office was so beige he almost blended into the walls. But was he a good accountant you might be wondering. I guess he was because I worked with him for a period of time. However, the experience was so unsatisfying that I don't actually know if he was skilled or not as the experience always left a bad taste in my mouth. He seemed to do the work I needed him to do, however I avoided meetings with him if possible, and when I did wind up having a meeting with him, I felt so disconnected that I couldn't speak freely, and because of that I wasn't really getting value out of the time I spent with him.

Needless to say, I eventually found an accountant that I resonated with. In fact, I greet my current accountant with a hug. In this case the exchange of energy between us is productive, fulfilling for both of us, and it's one of the reasons that I've become loyal to her and refer others to her as well.

I dare say you've felt the impact someone else's energy has had on you in some way in a personal or business setting. But have you ever audited your own energy levels? Maybe you've never even given the question of energy a second thought. You wouldn't be the only one in that camp I promise you. They say that knowledge is power, so now you have the power to make a real difference in your business and your life through managing your energy.

THE IMPORTANCE OF ENERGY

I started playing with this notion of energy with my clients when I first got a handle on how important it is in the business context. As a person with high functioning anxiety, my energy levels can be naturally very high or very low with not much in between. So I continually make an effort to consciously control my energy to get the most out of each experience with my staff or clients.

Of course, I took a different approach to client interactions than I took with my staff. With clients I was conscious of not being that annoying loud over the top so and so with the crazy high energy that I know is a part of me that could easily show up. So, what I started doing was consciously matching their energy. What I mean by that is that I would do my best to read their energy and then match it and add about 10% more positivity. For example, if a client walked in and I started with a "good morning, how are you?" and they just nodded or grunted, I'm not going to launch into a high energy conversation about the latest AFL game or the weather. That would probably annoy them. Instead, I would interact with them pleasantly and efficiently while getting straight into whatever matter of business they'd come in for.

The question of energy and tone even matters in written communication. For example, if I was working for a first home buyer when an important milestone has been reached in the purchasing process, then the email to them would include wording like:

> *Congratulations! We are so pleased to let you know .....*
> *You can expect the next time for us to check in with you to be ..... but please do reach out at any time if you have a query.*
> *We are so pleased to be on this journey with you.*

What's important to note here is that if I was to set that tone and wording as a template to be used for every client indiscriminately, there would inevitably be a mismatch of energy in some cases.

For example, a developer who is selling 200 blocks of land a year doesn't need the kind of nurturing messaging that a first time home owner would really appreciate. It could even backfire by giving them the impression that we've failed to understand them and their needs. For these clients, what works best is a direct and professional approach like:

> *We are pleased to confirm ….*
> *We will be in contact again when ….*

What I've learnt over the years I've been in business is not only that my energy is in the spotlight, but that it has more influence on my team than I imagined it would. This doesn't mean we have to be high energy and positive all the time. I say that because it's important to be authentic. Having positive energy doesn't mean we can't show our stress and the effects of running a business. In fact, acknowledging that our energy is a bit low with the team whenever it is, will result in their appreciating your trust in them and your transparency. If you're wondering what you could say, I've provided a couple of examples of the kinds of things I've said to my team in the past here.

> *Hi team, I am just a little flat today after a long night finishing off the end of month accounts, so don't worry, nothing's wrong. I'm actually looking forward to getting on with x, y, and z now that the accounts are behind me.*

Another option could be -

> *Sorry if I seem out of sorts today. Internally I am smiling, but I am just going to be head down and bum up getting this important task done for a while.*

If you adopt a similar approach, you will be relieved of the stress of feeling like you always need to be in an up mood. I say that because your mood won't be misjudged and negatively impact the team.

I was a few years into my business when I started to notice that my unique value was in my energy. I got to see that it was my energy that attracts people. It also enables me to positively influence others because it makes them feel safe, connected, and important. In the world of being a business owner, having energy that creates a positive influence is gold when it comes to having staff who want to follow you. I say that because when they believe in the business vision and feel fulfilled in the knowledge that their work matters, they will naturally strive to do their best.

For clients, my energy helps them to feel safe, heard and understood. In turn, that builds their confidence in me because a real sense of trust and connection naturally happens. I attribute our clients becoming our biggest cheerleaders to that very fact. It was when I fully adopted the belief that my energy is my currency that things really changed for me. I say that because when I started protecting and leveraging my energy, I was able to take my life in general, and my business in particular to a whole other level.

So, you might be wondering what you need to do to use energy to your advantage. The first thing to know is that the key is awareness. It's about being aware of the way we're interacting with someone and how they are reacting to us. It comes right down to things like the tone of voice we communicate with, the words we use, the context we put around the things we say, the way we hold ourselves, and our ability to genuinely lean in and listen to the person we are dealing with.

Managing our energy effectively is also about being able to moderate our approach if we have a tendency to be over the top, really loud, or likely to come across as if we're trying to force our opinions on to the person we're interacting with. The thing is that communicating with others effectively while not chewing up all of our emotional energy in the process, doesn't come down to whether we're an introvert or an extrovert, or somewhere in between. I say that because while we all have natural inclinations, we also have the freedom to be intentional in our interactions with others. What that means is that we are responsible for managing the way we engage with people in a way the results in the influence we have being positive.

I suspect you can probably reflect on times when you've acted in a certain way and people just didn't connect with you, and other times when you were able to create a degree of influence and connection easefully and immediately. The bottom line is that it's being able to manage the results we achieve in this regard that makes the difference between the people who are awake to the importance of energy, and those who are not.

So, if you feel like you've just been woken up by reading this chapter, I'd urge you to start recognising the unique characteristics you have that people are drawn to. Meanwhile, if you find yourself struggling to get your head around what energy actually is, it might help you to think of it as the kind of 'vibes' someone gets when they're with you and vice versa. In other words, it's a conscious or unconscious sense people get about us when they're in our company.

This is important in business because trust is a core ingredient that's in the mix when it comes to the decisions people make about whether to work with us or not. The thing is that we can't just tell someone we're trustworthy. A track record of trust is created when we consistently do what we say we are going to do. It is reflected in our reputation, as well as the sense people get when they're with us. This is important because it's the sense of ease, trust and real connection that enables us to get an edge over our competitors through the influence our energy has on our current and potential clients.

This starts from the very first impression we make. What that comes down to is everything from the clothes we wear, the tone of our voice, the body language we give off, and the words we speak.

THE IMPORTANCE OF ENERGY

I truly believe the success of my business is attributable in no small part to the energy I generate both personally, and through the team I've built up around me. It's a simple as this - if people like us, they will want to work with us.

The key factor that goes into determining whether people like us or not is our ability to establish trust and make them feel safe, understood and confident about our ability to achieve the results they want. When we tick those boxes, people are not only a lot more likely to do business with us, but also to refer us to their family and friends.

The thing to note here is that when I talk about energy it's not a euphemism for customer service. Sure enough, excellent customer service is critical to running a successful business. Whereas energy both underlies and overarches customer service. I decided to consult the dictionary as I was writing this section to get my thoughts really clear. The Oxford Dictionary defines customer service as "the assistance and advice provided by a company to those people who buy or use its products or services." So with that in mind, I want you to know that energy determines how well we are able to deliver services to our clients.

Is there a time when you interacted with a client about the same product or service you'd been selling for years (so you know the territory and the product inside out), but your mood was low, and the transaction went badly? On the other hand, is there another time when you felt great and that was portrayed in the conversation and the transaction with a client for whom the product was no more suitable than it was in the other case, but the sale was made easefully without a hitch? That's the impact of energy.

I know you've already heard me say that being excellent at your craft alone is not enough in the context of running a business. Well that's also the case when it comes to brokering great results no matter where you sit in the chain of command. Yes, you will do well if you have the product knowledge and offer top quality service to your clients. But to really put the icing on the cake and to be at the top of your industry, you need to focus on your energy.

The best way to look at energy is to regard it as a tangible asset that should be given the credibility it deserves through the way you leverage it. The great thing about your energy is that it is unique to you. Therefore, leaning into your unique energy is the best way of connecting with your unique client base. You're not going to be offering the perfect solution for everyone, but if you start using your energy as an asset within your business, then you will be positioning yourself to attract and retain your ideal prospects.

Because energy is as important as it is, it goes without saying that we need to be mindful of preserving it. For lack of a better way of putting it, energy takes energy. We burn physical and mental energy in everything we do, that's just simple science. So if we are trying to leverage our version of personal energy for our business, we need to make sure we are not failing to practice self-care, and as a result of that, burning out.

It's nothing short of imperative that we make sure we are preserving and replenishing our energy in order to stay well in ourselves, and effective within our business. For my part, I'm hyper aware of the fact that I need to protect my energy fiercely, especially the older I get. Over the years I have had to make changes to my lifestyle to ensure my energy is at its best when I need it to be. I'm 44 as I'm writing this book, and the tools I use now for protecting my energy include:

- Regular meditation
- Mindful movement like yoga or walking - anything where I am not creating cortisol or stress
- Taking down-time including removing stimulation like TV and my phone at certain times throughout the day

- Simply not talking to people - I am naturally an extrovert, but I have learnt to schedule times where I'm a bit of a hermit to recover my energy and focus
- Reading fiction.

I included reading fiction above because while I love to learn and naturally read a lot of non-fiction books in the interest of my personal and professional development, it's reading fiction books that enables me to relax. That's when the part of my brain that's engaged in the learning of new concepts and ideation gets to take a break. I feel like reading fiction is tantamount to someone taking our brain on a journey without our needing to take any responsibility for where the journey takes us.

On a side note: I didn't read fiction for a long time because I figured that if I was going to go to the effort of reading, I wanted to make sure it was beneficial from the point of view of learning something. I'm glad I busted through that self-made myth because I've found that incorporating non-fiction into my life has increased my vocabulary, and there are some non-fiction books that have also taught me some important things. In fact, the first non-fiction book I read after finishing university was *Eleanor Oliphant is Completely Fine* which is a novel written by Gail Honeyman. It taught me about empathy, understanding and tolerance.

Even though I'm conscious of protecting my energy, I was heartened when I held a Q and A session on my Instagram page, and someone asked me how I always have such amazing energy. I smiled and thought – "it's working". The reason I raise this here is that no one can be high energy all the time. Meanwhile if people think you have energy all the time, then you must be managing it well. I say that because you obviously have it at your disposal when you need it. So just like everybody else, I most certainly don't have the kind of energy people equate me with all the time. I conserve it so that I can call on it when it matters.

I especially focus on how I turn up when I'm at work. This is important because my team feeds off my energy. If my energy is off – the mood in the office is down. If my energy is good – my staff are happy and productive. The thing is that being the leader of a team means we are in the spotlight and people pay more attention to our energy than they would if we were just another staff member. So it's important not to dilute the influence you have on your team's mood and effectiveness through the way you turn up.

I guess what I'm about to say goes without saying, but I'll say it anyway. Energy is just as important for your life outside of the context of dealing with clients. As I mentioned earlier, energy is important when it comes to the quality of the interactions you have with your team members who look to you for leadership, and of course it can't be ignored in relation to the people in your life outside of your business.

After years of understanding and respecting the importance of energy, there's no doubt in my mind that the energy I bring to the table (whether it's around my team, or during meetings with clients, or with family members and friends) has the potential to be much more impactful than my words. That's why the motto my staff and I have adopted as part of our ethos is that 'they will remember how we made them feel, not what we said'. This is especially true in the professional services industries. Clients don't want you to rattle off an encyclopedia of your knowledge in relation to the services you offer. They want to feel safe, heard, understood and provided with the information they need.

THE IMPORTANCE OF ENERGY

YOUR REFLECTIONS

- When have you felt your energy positively or negatively affected a business outcome?
- How do you manage your energy during a typical workday?
- Recall a situation where matching a client's energy proved effective. What was the outcome?
- Consider your daily routines. Which activities enhance your energy and which ones drain it?
- What tools could you introduce to protect your energy?

CHAPTER THREE:
The Advantage of Emotional Intelligence

Excellence is not an act, but a habit.

What I want you to take away from reading this chapter is an appreciation of the fact that developing emotional intelligence (also known as EI) is one of the most effective things you can do to prepare yourself to be successful in both your personal and professional life.

I have often said that I would have been a much more successful track cyclist if I had the emotional intelligence I have now. I say that because I was an excellent cyclist who was capable of breaking records. However, while the kinds of speeds I regularly achieved in training should have made me a champion, my mind got in the way and compromised my results when I was racing.

Much to my coach's disappointment, I continually achieved much faster times in training than I produced on race days. Unfortunately, anxiety reared its head and hindered my performance when I was racing. You might be wondering why I wasn't able to deal with my nerves better than that as an elite athlete. Well, the thing is that what I was dealing with was much more severe than nerves. It was pure anguish and lack of ability to control my emotions that seriously hindered my ability to perform at my best on race days.

The shame of it is that I simply didn't have the emotional maturity to handle my competitive spirit back then. What that meant was that I had to really dislike (or not even know) the people I was competing with to be fired up enough to beat them. In other words, I couldn't be friendly with any direct competitors because I would unconsciously sabotage myself to avoid the discomfort I would've experienced if I beat them.

The other thing that compromised my ability to be the best cyclist I could be was that I lacked the kind of emotional fortitude I needed to be able to benefit from the feedback my coaches were giving me. Back in those days, feedback was always a one-way street because what I needed most at the time was validation and reassurance. That's a shame, because in a sport like cycling where milliseconds are the difference between winning and losing, my inability to leverage and act on feedback doomed me to continually fall short of my goals and capacity.

That's not to say that I didn't win any of my races. In fact, I held a number of Australian Masters Championship records. That said, I left way too many achievements I could have had under my belt unrealised because of the state of my mindset, and relative lack of emotional intelligence. I knew it, and my coaches knew it too. It was my coach telling me that I was 'the biggest underperformer he had ever known' that proved to be the turning point in my cycling career. Looking back on it now, I know he said that to motivate me. However, at the time it did just the opposite. It both crushed me, and affirmed what I already knew.

The silver lining in all of this is that my fascination with the power of connection, human interaction, and emotional intelligence was born out of the frustration my situation in the world of cycling generated. Basically, I took all the good things like the application of discipline, achieving a competitive edge, and leveraging the value of marginal gains, and used them to be the best I could be in my conveyancing and mentoring businesses. This matters to me because I'm committed to making a real difference to the clients I serve.

I'm proud to say that I run my business as well as I do as a result of the high performing team I nurture and inspire by example. I believe that any high performing team, whether in business or in sport, must embody the key components required for success. As I see it, those key components are strong leadership, individual accountability, and a collaborative spirit. For my own part, in addition to ticking those boxes, I put my success down to a commitment to continual learning and maintaining a focus on emotional intelligence.

What I want you to know is that I didn't get to where I am now without investing in my personal development. The kinds of professionals I've engaged in the fields of coaching, counselling, hypnotherapy and psychology have played a significant part in the success I am achieving now. I have always been driven by results, but it was only when I started working on myself, that I started to see how great the results I could generate could actually be.

Among other things, learning how to communicate more effectively, and how to control my emotions plays a big part in my ability to make a positive difference to the wellbeing and effectiveness of my team. These are the kinds of things that form the foundations for success that I base the way I live, and how I run my business on these days. I believe that it is the mastery of interpersonal relationships and a high level of emotional intelligence, married with my experience as an athlete that continues to arm me with a huge competitive edge.

Looking back on it now, I can see that track cycling was a selfish sport. I guess it had to be. When it came to cycling, I had to be focused on what I could get out of each and every situation. These days, my focus is on what I can contribute to each and every situation. I find this to be a far more fulfilling place to come from. That's probably because I find people really fascinating. That's why

I continually increase my capacity to be effective through things like getting accredited as an Everything DiSC and Trust Inside facilitator.

I smile when I think about the fact that it's my background in cycling that has made me a better business owner and leader. I had poor mental health and little ability to handle emotions effectively when I was focused entirely on cycling. However, more than anything else, it is my weaknesses that the personal and professional development I've done since retiring my cycling career has led to my strengths. This is one of the major factors I attribute my business success to.

So, although I never managed to achieve the heights in cycling that I know I was physically capable of, I'm grateful for the way things have panned out. I say that because failing to dominate in the arena of cycling was the catalyst for the level of success I am experiencing in my business and my life more generally right now. As my great friend and mentor Peter Cook reminded me of when I talked to him about this, "I did the best that I could with the tools I had at the time".

That's enough about me though, because I want you to really grasp what emotional intelligence is and how you can develop it. So by way of a definition, emotional intelligence refers to the ability to recognise, understand, manage, and reason with emotions in oneself and others. It involves a set of skills that help people to navigate the emotional aspects of life, improve their communication skills, empathise with others, overcome challenges. and defuse conflict. The bottom line is that emotional intelligence is pivotal for personal and professional success, as it affects how we manage our behaviour, navigate social complexities, and make personal decisions that achieve positive results.

Daniel Goleman is the author of *Emotional Intelligence: Why it can matter more than IQ*. Goleman's framework on emotional intelligence details four key domains. They are self-awareness, self-management, social awareness, and relationship management.

According to Goleman, self-awareness is the ability to recognise and understand our own emotions and their influence on our thoughts and actions. It entails understanding our strengths and areas for improvement, and fostering self-confidence. While self-management is about regulating our emotions, controlling impulses, responding to situations with emotional stability, showing initiative, honouring our commitments, and effectively adapting to change. Social awareness entails the capacity to grasp and empathise with the emotions, needs, and concerns of others, perceiving emotional cues, navigating social environments with ease, and understanding the dynamics within groups and/or organisations.

Last but not least, Goleman emphasizes that relationship management is critical, and that it entails communicating effectively, motivating and influencing others, collaborating as part of a team, and adeptly handling conflicts. What I want to add here is that developing emotional intelligence is a continuous process that involves a commitment to self-improvement. So here are some strategies you could implement to kick off and/or enhance your emotional intelligence:

1. **Practice self-awareness**: Spend time reflecting on your emotions and the impact they have on your decisions and actions. Keeping a journal can be a helpful way to track your emotional triggers and patterns.
2. **Improve self-management**: Once you are aware of your emotions, work on managing them. Techniques such as deep breathing, meditation, or even something as simple as taking a long walk can help you calm down and think more clearly when you're faced with stressful situations.
3. **Enhance social awareness**: Try to see things from the perspectives of others and cultivate empathy. Pay attention to things like body language, facial expressions, and tone of voice to better understand what others are feeling.

4. **Work on your people skills**: Effective communication skills including active listening, and showing appreciation to others can strengthen our relationships. Also, being open to feedback and addressing conflicts constructively can improve your interpersonal skills.
5. **Seek feedback**: Getting honest feedback from trusted friends, family, or colleagues can provide insights into areas that need improvement.
6. **Engage in professional development**: I'd recommend you consider taking courses or workshops focused on emotional intelligence. These can provide structured learning and practical exercises to enhance your acuity in relation to using your emotions in positive ways.

I feel confident in saying that by consciously working on these areas, you will be able to enhance your effectiveness in general and your emotional intelligence in particular. This will not only position you to be much more successful in your business or profession. It will also enable you to enjoy and maintain more meaningful relationships, and increase your wellbeing overall.

YOUR REFLECTIONS

- What are your strengths when it comes to EI?
- Where could you improve your EI?
- What impact would that have on your business?
- Which of the six strategies would have the biggest impact for you?
- What professional development could you do?

PART TWO:
Team

CHAPTER FOUR:
The Value of Support

Empower others to magnify your impact.

I opened my business because I was a great conveyancer and I wanted to take a leap of faith and see if I could go it alone. This kind of motivation is a common theme that comes up when I talk to other first-time business owners. Like I did, they opened their business because they wanted to have more control over what they were doing. They are also passionate about their craft, they wanted more flexible working hours, and more creative freedom.

As I mentioned in the introduction, to this day I am yet to meet anyone who opened their first business because they were good at running a business. What's more, in the excitement of going out on our own, most of us completely overlook the things in the background that keep businesses afloat. It would be a beautiful thing if it wasn't the case, but as anyone who took the leap without being prepared found out sooner rather than later, in most cases running a business takes very different skills to those involved in the craft the business is focused on.

When I was at university there wasn't a single subject on running or managing a business available as part of the curriculum. The closest thing were the accounting subjects, but these were solely based on trust accounting. In other words, they covered the responsibilities of handling and/or managing other people's money. Sadly, there was nothing that covered topics like marketing, budgeting and reporting, or human resource management.

The problem is that not so long after opening our business we discover that we need to be a human resource specialist, a bookkeeper, a sales and marketing expert – and the list goes on! Even though it might feel overwhelming, many people in business that I've spoken to are like I was before I saw the light. Like me, they assumed they should just bite the bullet and work out how to do all of the new tasks they've had no training in whatsoever.

To this day, I still can't understand what's behind the thought processes of the small business owners who believe they have to do everything on their own, even though I used to be one of them myself. Maybe it's about not wanting to admit they need help. I mean, after all they opened the business, therefore they should have all the answers, shouldn't they? A consequence of that assumption is that it would look like they're incompetent or lazy if they asked for help. On a more practical level though, it often comes down to a concern around not being able to afford to buy in assistance.

I remember what it's like struggling to see the benefits of paying for help in relation to tasks that don't have a direct financial impact on the income coming into the business. The bottom line is that the warped kind of heroism that can play out around going it alone is an invitation to things like burnout, the potential for serious and possibly costly errors to occur, and the ineffective use of our limited time.

I know it can be hard to see the forest for the trees when we're new to the business of running a business. I can tell you from first-hand experience that things like loneliness, burnout, and despair are real. What's more, there is a cost associated with having to deal with these things, especially burnout which can debilitate people for months or even years. The good news is that these things are avoidable. So, I beg you, please don't waste time and energy on trying to do everything on your own.

My top tips based on the things that have worked for me in terms of building a support network and avoiding the pitfalls of trying to do everything on my own, include:

1. **Joining local business networks**: Business associations, chambers of commerce, or business focussed networking groups often have regular meetings and provide a platform for connecting with other business owners who are keen to learn from and support each other.
2. **Engaging in online communities**: Participating in relevant online forums, and social media groups on platforms like LinkedIn can offer a wealth of knowledge, support, and virtual networking opportunities.
3. **Attending industry and networking events**: Conferences, workshops, and seminars are great places to meet peers, learn new skills, and find potential collaborators and/or mentors.
4. **Seeking and offering mentoring**: Engaging a mentor is a great way to access guidance, support, and insight from someone who has gone before us. On the other hand, offering mentoring to others can be incredibly rewarding and beneficial in relation to the way we are positioned in our area of expertise.
5. **Collaborating with other businesses**: Collaborating with complementary businesses can lead to shared resources including networks, referrals, and mutual support around business and personal development.
6. **Hiring a business coach**: A business coach can provide personalised advice and help us navigate the challenges of running a business, including how to effectively build a network.
7. **Staying open to learning**: There's no question of the value of attending training sessions, webinars, and courses to continue acquiring new skills and learning more generally. In addition to professional development, attending courses and joining industry forums is a great way to meet people and remain abreast of the latest trends and best practices in your industry.

On the basis of my own experience, my sense is that the above tips will have more leverage for those who operate in smaller regional communities. I say that because it seems to be easier to build rapport and trust as part of a smaller community, whereas in the larger metro areas there's more potential for people like us to become just a number. In either case, what I know for sure is that there is strength in being vulnerable and seeking out help and companionship when we're running a business. I say that because as humans we're built for connection with others. What that means is that isolating ourself when things might not be going so well is the worst thing business people can do from the point of view of their mental health. It also hinders their ability to get out of the hole they've found themselves in.

Engaging a Mentor:
These days I proudly tell people I have a mentor. What's more, I'm pretty sure I always will. This hasn't always been the case though. When I first opened my business, I had trouble getting my head around what having a mentor would look like, and what I would get out of it. In fact, in the early days when I eventually started working with a mentor, I kept pretty quiet about it because of a warped sense of being seen as weak because I needed mentoring. Then once I got to experience the benefits of being mentored, I went through a stage of not telling anyone about it because I wanted to keep it as my secret weapon that gave me a distinct competitive edge.

The paradox is that during my cycling career it would have been unheard of for someone who was serious about being competitive not to have a coach. In fact, it's not unusual for those at the top of their game to have multiple coaches/mentors. In my own case, I had a cycling coach and a strength and conditioning coach, as well as having people advising me on nutrition and mindset. It's simply a given that people with athletic careers will have a coach/s and mentor/s. It's a no brainer really. So what I want you to know is that there's no question that surrounding yourself with people who have the experience and capacity to bring out the best in you will make the world of difference.

I kicked myself when I got to see the light after years of struggling without the kind of support that is readily available in the form of business mentors and coaches. The way I wound up working with my first mentor was almost by accident. I engaged a friend of a friend who was a habit coach to keep me accountable when it came to my health. This came about when the penny dropped and my attention was drawn to the fact that since wrapping up my cycling career and opening my business, I had been prioritising my business over my health. Of course, I already knew the things I should be doing in the way of exercise and nutrition, but I'm sorry to say that looking after my health fell victim to my business taking precedence over everything else.

The first step I took in the right direction was to follow the advice I got from Amanda who was the habit coach I engaged. She helped to keep me accountable for things like regularly getting my steps in by walking every day. It's not surprising that a very strong friendship developed between Amanda and I because we had both spent time at the elite level of our respective sports. In her case it was high performance basketball.

Eventually the kind of coaching I was getting from Amanda reached its use by date. That said, we are still connected because we have become great friends. I will always be grateful to Amanda because working with her woke me up to the fact that even outside of the sporting arena, we can all benefit from enlisting help to reach our goals and take our business and our life to a whole other level.

These days, far from being embarrassed about not knowing it all, I know that engaging a coach or mentor of some kind is an incredibly smart strategic move that high achievers don't give a second thought to. I've actually had a few business mentors over the years. At times I've had a couple at the same time working on specific projects and/or different aspects of my business. As I mentioned earlier, more recently I've had the great good fortune of having my dear friend Peter Cook as my mentor.

I consider myself to be incredibly lucky to have Pete as a mentor. It's not only that I get to call him, his wife and his two beautiful girls my extended family now. On the professional side of things, what being mentored by Pete provides me with is someone to help me look at things objectively. He does that by asking me the kinds of questions good mentors are skilled at asking to help their clients find the answers within themselves. In many ways, he's like a whiteboard for my thoughts to be critiqued on, and an advocate who supports me through thick and through thin.

Since working with Pete, I've been brave enough to make huge strategic decisions including launching my conveyancing business in Victoria after 10 years of limiting our services to New South Wales. I've also got him to thank for the fact that I've written this book, set up a mentoring practice of my own, created an overseas outsourcing model, launched a speaking career delivering key notes, and so much more.

90% of the time it's not a case of Pete telling me something I don't already know. He just asks me the right questions so that I get to find the answers myself. Arguably, I could have achieved many of the results I've brokered during my time with Pete as my mentor without his guidance. But I am certain I would not have achieved them in the same time frame or with the degree of ease I have. I say that because the biggest change I've noticed since working with Pete is the dramatically increased levels of clarity, confidence and focus that I have.

What I want to stress here is that there's no doubt in my mind that it's taking my relationship with my mentor as seriously as I do, that has a lot to do with the fact that our working relationship has been as successful as it has. Among other things, I treat the time I spend in the mentoring relationship with the utmost respect. What this means is that I make sure I am as prepared for my sessions with Pete as possible.

What you need to be aware of is that a mentor will never do the work for you. What they will do is give you the nudge, the confidence, and the guidance to get you going. I am blessed to have such a quality mentor not only because my business has gone ahead in leaps and bounds since I've been working with him, but also my experience as a mentee with a top-class mentor has enabled me to model the best of the best and refine my skills as a mentor. What's more, Pete is also an Ishaya Monk and has taught me how to meditate. So he has also become an accountability buddy and spiritual adviser in relation to my meditation practice. This dance between Pete being my business mentor, meditation adviser and also close personal friend has created a high degree of trust that makes our time together invaluable.

I have plenty to be grateful for, that's for sure. That's why I've resolved to have a mentor forever. Sure, Pete might not know everything, but he knows me and that means he is able to help me achieve more than I could ever achieve on my own.

My Journey to Becoming a Business Mentor:
Becoming a business mentor was not something I had planned. I'd even go so far as to say that I used to be slightly averse to the word mentor. When I was rebranding my business in 2018, my branding consultant Colette suggested I use the words 'property conveyance mentor' in my title. At that time, using the word mentor was unheard of in our industry. I have to admit I wasn't as open minded back then as I am now, and I was reluctant to stick my neck out because what Colette was suggesting was so different to the norm.

Colette brought me around on the basis of the fact that the title 'property conveyance mentor' eliminated any sense of us being on a pedestal telling our clients what to do. This is important because that's not what people get when they work with us. What they get is professionals who are totally invested in the outcomes they achieve and the confidence they have in the choices they ultimately make. So, in other words, we are there to guide and support our clients the whole way through buying and/or selling a property, or not (as the case may be).

The whole branding exercise was a fantastic experience, and there's a lasting legacy in a tag line that came out of my numerous conversations with Colette that fits us to a T. The tag line is that 'we'll walk you home'. This approach we take is so different to what it was like back in the day when I worked in law firms. In contrast, there was a feeling of muted (and sometimes not even muted) arrogance in the air. It was as if we were doing our clients a favour by acting on their behalf. Essentially, dealing with customers in the firms I worked with was just a transaction. There was no time for warmth or empathy in an environment like the one I was working in. It was about getting the job done, charging by the minute, and meeting our KPI's. The culture was embedded in an ethic of transactions first and relationships second.

Things couldn't be more different now. In my business we prioritise relationships over transactions. This means we live and breathe the importance of the quality of the interactions we have with our clients every day. It was conversations around these behaviours that tweaked Colette's creative mind to the extent that the idea of calling myself a 'property conveyance mentor' came up. I took action on that idea and essentially rebranded myself, but not without experiencing a bit of backlash. Interestingly, there was absolutely no negative feedback coming from my clients. However, two local conveyancing businesses took particular offence. One posted a snide comment on social media on top of a post of mine where I talked about being a property conveyancing mentor. Another local conveyancing businessowner put a laughing emoji on one of my posts, and then reshared it on their page. This is just a taste of the kind of passive aggressive behaviour that our rebranding elicited from some of our competitors.

Rather than taking this kind of thing to heart, I saw it as a brilliant example of projection. I found out about the phenomenon of projection when I first started working with a mentor. It explains some of the otherwise inexplicable behavior we see and even display from time to time. Essentially, projection is our way of dealing with feelings we're not ready to own yet. And because we can't own those feelings, we project them onto others. As a result of the work I've done on myself, I know that more often than not, when a competitor lashes out at my business it comes from the fact that they're feeling threatened.

The thing is that I've never thought of myself as a disruptor, but apparently, I am. I say that because the more dynamic and successful I became, the more back lash I experienced. More importantly though, business was really booming, and I was starting to get noticed. In fact, in 2019 I won the prestigious Australian Institute of Conveyancers (NSW) President's Award. When I was interviewed after winning the award I was quoted as saying "I won because of my passion and drive to modernise our industry in a way that puts conveyancers at the forefront of the consumer's mind. The Award recognises my hard work over nine and a half years to ensure that I was leading the way in e-Conveyancing, mentoring, and client-centric experiences."

The impact of this was immediate. I say that because before the awards night was even over, I had a number of people who ran conveyancing businesses reaching out to me asking for advice. All I heard for the rest of the night was the way people were loving the client centric way of doing business I had created. Some of those people were also talking about possibly working with me to shore up their success in this new modern era where the primacy of the customer experience is the difference that makes the difference.

It didn't stop there though. The Australian Institute of Conveyancers (NSW) then engaged me to speak at two of their events. One was their annual state conference which is the pinnacle event they run every year. This was an interesting challenge for me. Not only had I never delivered a keynote before, but I was also the first conveyancer to speak at this prestigious event. My presentation was all about embracing our uniqueness to achieve business success. In it I shared all of my secrets, from the social media plans I instituted, to our strategy around dressing differently, to the language we use, and everything in between that I'd done with my business to disrupt the status quo.

Some of my colleagues questioned why I would give away this kind of information to people who are essentially my competitors. They missed the point really because my uniqueness is different to anyone else's. And if anyone copied me, then they would always be one step behind me.

On the night in question, I was incredibly bold and inspired with the intention of empowering the sold-out room in front of me to be more curious in relation to the way they do things. Or in other words, I wanted them to give themselves permission to step outside of the square and stop worrying about doing things a certain way because that's what's expected of them. I must have hit a nerve because I was inundated with other conveyancers asking me for my help during the cocktail function that followed my keynote. Requests were still flowing in when I got back to Albury where I'm based.

So notwithstanding the energy around the haters I mentioned earlier, I more or less easefully fell into the role of becoming a business mentor. When people ask me what I did to make this happen while maintaining the success of the conveyancing side of my business, I say that it comes down to three fundamental factors. They are that I never stopped focusing on being my authentic self, I was consistent in relation to staying in my own lane, and I never took my foot off the pedal when it came to the question of how I could change the way I did business to be even more impactful.

At the time, I was running one to one mentoring sessions with conveyancers across the state. I also had a group mentoring program called 'Bold Moves to Win Big in Business' which I sold to different industries. The beauty of it is that my insights aren't just effective for the conveyancing industry. These 'bold moves' as I call them are dynamic skills and disruptive thinking processes that would work for anyone in business.

The personal growth I experienced during this time was invaluable. Not only was I becoming incredibly fulfilled, but I also realised that I really loved helping people. In fact, I feel blessed to be part of a community supporting each other and simply being of service.

When Covid hit, I took a break from business mentoring because the conveyancing side of my business needed my full attention. I was actually happy to step back into the trenches of the conveyancing business at the time, even if it meant pulling back on things like mentoring and delivering keynotes. These were unprecedented times. My first love, the conveyancing business needed me because many of the workflows and templates we had so carefully curated were redundant. That related to the fact that Covid required a new way of running a business. So I stopped mentoring and threw all my energy into supporting the business and my employees during Covid. It was the right decision at the right time.

Among other things, the property market was booming, and we were as busy as ever when the restrictions around Covid were lifted. I had people reaching out for mentoring, but I'd kind of got used to not doing it to be honest. That's until the owners of my yoga studio invited me to have dinner with them in December 2021. So, I went to dinner with the owners who had become friends, and I soon discovered the purpose of the dinner was for them to ask if I would mentor them.

I was caught a little off guard, but I could see a lot of untapped potential in their business and decided to put them on a six-month retainer, and the rest is history. I'm grateful to those lovely ladies from my yoga studio who sparked my love of mentoring again. I had forgotten how beautiful it feels to be able to help people in areas outside of conveyancing. It reminded me that for otherwise sometimes lonely business owners, having a sounding board and a support system to take their business to a place where they can absolutely thrive is invaluable.

Through all of this I kept learning. Not long after finishing up with the yoga ladies, I was trained up to become an Everything DiSC Facilitator, and a Trust Inside Assessor. I also went through the 'High Performance Leaders' program with arguably Australia's best culture experts called 'Leading Teams'. I'm driven to keep learning because if there is one thing I know, it's that competence feeds confidence. I say that because the more skills I learnt, the more confident I felt in the role of a business mentor.

I am justified in my confidence as a business mentor because my methods are not merely theoretical, they are borne out of tried and tested strategies in my own business. This direct experience enables me to apply real-time, real-life feedback.

Among other things, I guess what I'm getting at here is that my conveyancing business is a testament to the value I'm able to offer as a business mentor. I think one of the other reasons people are drawn to me is that I show so much of the reality of being a business owner on my social media channels. In other words, people get a very genuine take on who I am, what I stand for, and how I do things.

These days I consciously split my working time up so that I focus 50% of my energy on business mentoring, 20% on conveyancing, and 30% focusing directly on the leadership aspects of my responsibilities within my conveyancing business. That was the ideal ratio I set out to achieve in 2022, and within one year I managed to reach it without any financial disadvantage to the conveyancing business.

What I love about mentoring is that it's a total win-win scenario. It creates bonds for me that have a positive impact on my life and the life of the people I work with. Not to mention the satisfaction I get out of seeing the concrete business and personal development related results they get out of it as well. This is also why I'm so choosy about who I work with in the business mentoring space.

The way I see it, turning people who don't resonate with me down is as respectful to them as it is to myself. I say that because I believe a big part of the effectiveness of the mentor/mentee relationship comes through having a true connection. Basically, if I wouldn't want to have a wine (or two) with someone who contacts me about mentoring, and/or if they lack a growth mindset, I won't work with them. I also have to believe in their purpose. I don't put it as bluntly as this when I talk to people seeking mentoring of course, but I'm strict on these parameters because I don't want to waste any of my time or their money.

You might be surprised to know that the majority of my clients are not conveyancers. I started to steer away from conveyancers some time ago because a lot of the people in that field who approached me were wanting to go into the mechanics and operations of being a conveyancer. That's not what I'm about these days, and they should have learnt those skills at university. My mentoring is based on the dynamic skills required to be successful in business, not the mechanics of the trade or craft. That's what apprenticeships, colleges and universities are for.

What I'm all about is helping my clients to take their business and their life to a whole other level through the changes they make as a person in the course of the work we do together. One of the most personally rewarding programs I run is called 'The Edge High Performance Leadership'. It involves a group of up to 10 non-competing businesses who come together once a month. The sessions within this program are comprised of a mixture of content, learning, sharing, feedback and networking.

The feedback I regularly receive from participants of this program is that they get a whole lot more value out of the insight into what others are experiencing than they would if they were signed up to a one on one arrangement. I understand where they're coming from because the environment I've set up creates a remarkable bond of camaraderie, support, and inspiration. I never take a one size fits all approach though. That's why I also offer one on one arrangements.

I totally love the conveyancing side of my business, and I feel blessed to have found a sweet spot with the mentoring side of it as well. I say that because while I love seeing my clients kicking goals they never would have dreamed they'd be able to achieve, I get to learn what does and doesn't work through the way my clients respond to the experience of working with me in the context of a group setting as well.

YOUR REFLECTIONS

- Who are the biggest supporters in your business?
- Where do you need more support in your business?
- How does your current approach to seeking support reflect your readiness to grow and adapt as a business owner?
- What might be the long-term impact on your business if you were to enhance your support network?
- Which of the support strategies mentioned in this chapter do you feel would most significantly benefit your current business situation?

CHAPTER FIVE:
The Power of Relationships

Prioritise relationships, not transactions.

Without a doubt, one of the keys to my success in life and in business is my focus on building strong and genuine relationships.

Let me share a story with you about what I went through when I first went out on my own and started my business. It was 2009, and within the first year of trading my previous employer initiated legal action against me with the view to restricting my ability to trade. It was a pretty tough way to kick things off, that's for sure. Let's just say that I wouldn't recommend anyone spending the first 12 months of their business knee deep in a crippling court case. It chewed up most of my energy, all of my money, and the majority of my time. It also played a significant part in the marital divorce I went through soon after the dust settled on the case.

Don't worry, this is not going to turn into a 'poor me' fest, or a 'bugger them' rant where I lash out about my previous employer. This is actually a story about the difference being part of a wonderful business community has made in the good and the not so good times. Long story short, as a result of my prioritising relationships, copious amounts of support flowed back to me from my business community during the court case that could have easily debilitated me without the kind of support I had. The result of this was that an event that could have otherwise resulted in the demise of my business turned into a situation that actually catapulted its success.

I smile when I think about the fact that the level of support I received from the business community during this time was worth much more than the $70,000.00 I paid out in legal fees. Though it didn't feel like it at the time, within months of the legal battle being finalised, I could see that it was probably the best start in business a person like me could ask for.

You're probably wondering why I would make a crazy statement like that given that the episode almost sent me broke, and came close to breaking my spirit as well. The answer to that question is that the support I received from my community sped up the trajectory of my business faster than I could have imagined. The thing is that the whole episode got my clients and business contacts fired up about referring as much work to me as possible. Even with a $70,000.00 legal debt to deal with, I still managed to achieve a substantial profit that year. In fact, my client base was so healthy that I needed to engage my first employee within 6 months of opening the doors.

In my experience, there are a number of factors that contributed to my ability to build relationships like this. They are:

1. Showing genuine interest and care for others.
2. Being loyal and diligent in relation to keeping an eye out for opportunities to pass on to people in our network.
3. Focusing on staying relevant. In other words, don't bug people for the sake of connecting. Only contact them with things that are relevant to them.
4. Avoid talking about yourself the whole time. A wise person once said that we have two ears and one mouth, and we should use them accordingly.

The great thing about strong relationships is that they can endure challenges, and the people within them will stand firm in the face of temporary disruptions. This is possible because on some level those involved understand the dynamics at play and remain mindful of the feelings of the other person or people.

What I've discovered during my time in business is that remarkable individuals plan for what lies ahead, and allow for contingencies. They remember and honor those who've supported them previously, and they acknowledge the invaluable contributions others make to their business and/or life.

During a rebranding process I went through in 2019, my brand strategist asked me what made me so good at what I do. My answer was that "I find people fascinating". These words rolled off my tongue so easefully that it became a sort of motto I live by now. What that means is that I'm much more interested in what makes the other person tick than showing off about my achievements or pushing my opinion down anyone's throat. I'm also genuinely curious about what makes people think and react the way they do as they move through their life.

A by-product of this approach is that I don't have to work hard at establishing genuine connections with the people I meet because it is second nature to me. This in turn leads to the easeful forging of deeper and more meaningful relationships. What underlies this result is having a better understanding of the nature and values of the other person through the inquisitive approach I take with everyone I meet. Additionally, I naturally approach interactions with an open mind and an open heart. I often talk to the clients I'm mentoring about this topic, especially when they comment on the fact that I seem to know them better than they know themselves (or words to that affect). There's no doubt in my mind that this comes about because being focussed on people with fascination has several benefits for the person involved. These include:

1. **Feeling valued:** When you interact with someone with a framework of fascination energising you, it will enable you to easefully pay genuine attention to them. This makes the individual feel seen, heard, and valued. Those three words (seen, heard, and valued) punch well above their weight in

terms of the strength and integrity of the relationships we can build with this approach, especially in business. Basically, everyone wants to feel as if they matter, and this approach certainly meets that need.

2. **Increasing self-esteem:** Being considered interesting by another person can boost one's confidence and sense of self-worth. Among other things it validates their experiences and perspectives, and it reinforces the fact that they matter and deserve to be respected.
3. **Opening opportunities for self-reflection:** Because this approach involves asking open questions and expressing genuine interest, the person you're dealing with is afforded with an opportunity to reflect on their experiences and perhaps see themself in a new light.
4. **Feeling comfortable expressing themselves:** Knowing that they're being listened to without judgment encourages people to express themselves more openly and authentically.
5. **Strengthening relationships:** Because of the open and empowering communication that takes place in a situation involving interacting with fascination, stronger bonds are formed through trust and deeper understanding.
6. **Feeling accepted:** Really leaning in and listening to another person's stories and experiences can help people to feel like they are being accepted and valued for who they are. Being in an environment where this is the case can be deeply comforting.
7. **Finding it easier to open up:** People who feel valued and heard within a relationship will be more inclined to share deeper insights, stories, and feelings. This leads to richer and more meaningful conversations and relationships with others.
8. **Becoming empowered:** Showing an interest in someone's experiences (especially the ones that they are proud of, and/or define them) can empower them to recognise how great they are and encourage them to expect and strive for the best for and from themselves.

I've found the ability I have to focus on people with fascination to be a huge advantage in several respects. Dealing with difficult interactions with conveyancing clients that come up from time to time is a great example of the benefits of using this tool successfully. What I've found is that being open and non-judgmental enables me to find an appreciation for these clients, and treat them in a way that leaves them in no doubt about having been seen and heard. And without the potential heat that could otherwise make these interactions unproductive (or worse), we're able to work through whatever needs to be addressed for the client to be satisfied.

There have been a couple of times when I've found myself in a really heated situation with a person who starts off being defensive and argumentative. In these cases, I've resisted trying to fight fire with fire. Instead, I've made sure that I remain really present, and listen intently to what they had to say in a way that validated who they are and what their 'problem' is. Among other things, this approach took all of the heat out of the interaction and helped the person calm down and feel safe. When that was the case, we were able to work through the issue at hand without emotions hijacking the agenda.

You see, success in the broadest sense of the word is all about perspective. What I was doing in the example above was demonstrating empathy, being patient, and remaining present so that I wasn't triggered. The result of this was that we avoided a scenario that could have easily turned into a shouting match where the only thing the people involved have is 'a problem'. In my case, it would have been a problem with a difficult client, and in their case, it would have been whatever complaint they turned up to have a fight with me about. Whereas the approach I always take can turn a potentially ugly interaction into a situation where two people are working together to find 'a solution'.

I don't want to give you the impression that I'm unrealistically optimistic or naive in these kinds of situations though. Some people are just so deeply entrenched in an attitude of fight or flight that the best we can do is take a deep breath and hear them out. The important thing is not to be triggered by the behaviour that's generated through someone else's reactions.

Managing Our State:
The bottom line is that one of the most important relationships we have is the one we have with ourselves. You'll recall a moment ago that I mentioned handling myself in difficult situations in a way that enabled the client to feel as if they're really being seen and heard. Well as important as that is, maintaining balance matters. That's why not defaulting to people pleasing and/or deciding it's easier to say nothing is the way to go. I say that because I believe it's important to treat ourselves with the same respect as we show others. In other words, it's not pushy to politely behave in a way that conveys an expectation of being respected.

That said, I don't want you to think I'm perfect. In fact, looking back over some of the interactions I've had with people, there are plenty of times where I've been guilty of showing off and talking too much. I wasn't even aware I was coming across that way at the time. However, looking back on it now with self-compassion I can see that these kinds of things are motivated by a lack of self-confidence.

I remember an occasion when I was advising a client of their options by giving them way too much information. On reflection, it's clear that I was trying to prove my worth by demonstrating how much I knew about conveyancing. I also compulsively filled in gaps in the conversation because I was uncomfortable with silence. Needless to say, this was a learning opportunity for me, rather than being a masterclass in effectiveness.

Among other things, the problem with talking too much is that it doesn't allow any real depth to form in relationships. That's a shame because there's no doubt that we have the other person's interests at heart, but because we're not present, and we're worried about impressing them (whether they're conscious of it or not), they can feel that our focus is on ourself rather than them.

I'm providing a lot more information about managing our own state in the chapter on self-care that's coming up. So, to conclude this chapter, I want to urge you to not overlook the importance of investing time and effort into establishing genuine positive relationships with yourself and others. I'm passionate about this because it goes without saying that this approach is not only going to be beneficial from the point of view of your business, but also from the point of view of your wellbeing overall.

YOUR REFLECTIONS

- Which relationships have been most instrumental to the success of your business?
- How do you maintain strong connections during challenging times?
- Recall a recent client encounter. Did you prioritise the relationship or the transaction?
- How balanced is your approach between giving and receiving in professional relationships?
- What one change could you make to deepen the relationships within your business network?

CHAPTER SIX:
The Challenge of Leadership

Lead with vision, follow through with action.

Because I was a one-(wo)man band when I first started my business, I did everything. I opened files, I answered calls, I handled the mail and banking, I even cleaned the toilet. I was literally self-employed. For most of us, that's how we get started. We decide to go out on our own because we are great at what we do, and for a variety of different reasons we decide we are better off working for ourselves. By necessity, our focus is on the day-to-day tasks of the business.

In the beginning, I had no intention of growing my business and having employees. My plan was simply to be self-employed. Then I started to get really busy because an inevitable biproduct of doing an excellent job was that more and more work was being referred to me. After a while, the long hours were building up to a point where I was spending the odd night sleeping at the office.

Finally, I gave in to the fact that it was time to hire some help. Petrified of the risks involved in putting someone on, I started with a part time junior before progressing her into a traineeship. Hiring a young 18-year-old on a traineeship felt like the lowest risk option that was open to me at the time. I was more comfortable with the idea of covering the much lower wage than I would have to pay an experienced professional. Additionally, the trainee would be employed through a registered training organisation. That mattered because as the host employer, the option of finishing the trainee up earlier than planned if they didn't work out was available to me.

My focus here was around getting help and keeping my overheads low. There is definitely a time and place for keeping overheads low. Not having the discipline or awareness to do this is where startups can put the first nail in the coffin of their business. I know that's a pretty brutal way to put it, but the statistics around businesses closing down within the first five years are really telling. Meanwhile, while there is always merit in keeping overheads as low as practicable, in my own case the biggest problem was the overall approach I was taking.

At the time, I was operating with a task focused mindset, and even when I employed staff in the early days, I saw their job as helping me achieve the tasks I needed to. It never crossed my mind that I needed to become a leader. In fact, I am not even sure 29-year-old Peta even knew there was any difference between being self-employed and being a leader. I guess that's because I never experienced leadership or a culture of inclusive professional growth in any of the roles I'd previously held within law firms. About the only time we got to pause and take our focus off the grind of getting the work done back then, was when we all stopped work to watch the Melbourne Cup horse race on the TV. So, I guess what I'm saying is that back in those days I didn't know any different.

My first team member (let's call her Alice) was 18 when she started with me. The great thing about Alice is that she had a lot of drive right from day one. I was lucky to wind up with someone whose parents were entrepreneurs and business owners themselves, because among other things, Alice had two really important qualities. They were initiative and not being afraid of hard work. That was lucky because my idea of leadership in those early days was to advise Alice what tasks had to be done and explain how to do them – that was it. Among other things, I thought I needed to be a tough boss. There was no room for error and the client was always right at any expense.

How more wrong could I have possibly been?

Meanwhile the business got busier, and I employed more staff. Back in those days it was my business, and things were done my way because that's how I had always done them. Back then I was the conveyancer, and the staff were there to assist me to do the conveyancing work. My staff and I would work our butts off to get the job done and that was that.

Besides Alice, the first few years in my business had a pattern of new employees coming and going regularly. They seemed to burn out within 12-24 months and leave. On the other hand, Alice stayed for nine years. She was a resilient young woman and an excellent employee. I believe her work ethic and commitment had a lot to do with growing up in a family with parents who were hard workers.

Eventually the time came for me to take a moment to pause and take a long, hard, look at myself. On the surface, the facts were that I wasn't a bad person, on paper my business was successful, and we had a good slice of the local market share. So I couldn't understand why I wasn't able to hang on to employees for more than two years. Curiosity and love of learning led me to doing some personal and professional development around leadership. Through that I realised that I wanted to be the boss I wish I always had. What that meant was that I wanted to mentor employees while providing leadership and transparency so that they felt valued and respected. I wanted to create an environment where my staff had space to tap into their creativity and uniqueness. Then one day I came across this quote from Richard Branson:

> *Take care of your employees and they will take care of your business.*

This really resonated with me and sparked my curiosity about what it would look like if I shook up the way I approached my business. I had always put clients first. That meant that they were above my own personal needs, my marriage, and my employees. In other words, my entire focus was on the day to day running of my business. What that meant was that there was no management or development strategy of any kind in place. Things were about to change though because I started really thinking about what Branson's quote about taking care of our employees meant. This was the turning point where I transitioned from being self-employed to being a business owner who fully embraced the leadership responsibilities that came with that position.

The first thing I had to grapple with was a very practical matter. I had to work out how I was going to be able to start doing the kind of strategic thinking and working on leadership and culture required to build my business. The catch was that whatever approach I took had to allow for the money making activities that were sustaining the business at the time. The catch within the catch was that I was the only one who knew how to do the money making activities. In other words, I was faced with a structural problem when it came to the question of how I was going to be able to start working ON the business instead of IN the business?

The dilemma was real. If I wanted to have long term success, fulfillment, and a team of passionate and engaged staff, then I had to work out how to find time to do it in a way that didn't result in the volume or quality of work being sacrificed.

Then along came the book called *The E-Myth* by Michael E. Gerber. This was a game changer for me. Gerber's book addresses the fundamental misconceptions around starting and running a small business. One of the core messages in it is the importance of transitioning from being a technician who is deeply involved in the day-to-day technical tasks of their business, to adopting a more strategic approach.

Gerber talks about the fact that many business owners get trapped in the routine of working 'in' their business rather than investing time 'on' it. This means they're often caught up in immediate tasks and operations, rather than stepping back in order to plan, strategise, and build a system that can work independently of them.

"What - independently of me!" Hearing those words was a moment of truth for me. I can smile about it now, but among other things at that time, I hadn't had a holiday or a sick day in 6 years because things couldn't operate successfully without me.

The E-Myth was a great wakeup call that helped me to understand the importance of developing processes, delegating tasks, and focusing on the long-term growth and direction of my business. This is when I started transitioning from solely working in the business as a technician, to allocating time and headspace to focus on the business as an entrepreneur.

It might surprise you to know that I looked at McDonalds to answer the questions I had around creating processes and procedures to future-proof my business so that anyone could step into any role and know what to do. Have you ever watched the employees at McDonalds? Every single one of them knows what to do. There are timers, systems, alarms, and workflow protocols everyone is aware of. It can look like chaos when it's really busy, but if you stop and actually watch what's going on, you'll see that behind all the noise and fast pace of the operations, it's actually incredibly well organised. And most importantly, you could move any of those staff into any other role and things would still run at the same efficient pace.

Now that's what I call maximising efficiency and future proofing!

So, what I did first was systemising everything. There was no more keeping everything in my head because I was the boss and the only one who needed to be in the know. What rubbish! That was just a case of stroking my ego and not knowing any better. The problem was that I had created a workplace that needed me to run effectively because everything was kept in my head.

The kinds of things I did when I decided it was time for things to change included saving a letter that was being typed to go out to a client as a template so it could be used again and save time for anyone who needed to write a similar letter. I also created flow charts, and documented things like the way I handled difficult phone conversations so that my staff could refer to them when they had the same kind of issue to deal with.

In fact, pretty much any document that was prepared by my office was turned into a template, to avoid others having to recreate the same thing again and again. What pleasantly surprised me was that creating the processes and templates in real time didn't take that much time or energy.

It was a real eye opener for me when I realised how many of the tasks I'd been telling myself no-one else could do, actually resulted from my lack of patience and forward thinking in relation to systemising these tasks. My ego was probably in the way as well. The result of this realisation was that I started creating documents within a folder I called 'if, then, else'. These were documents that helped the team answer questions they might have otherwise had to refer to me instead. It is phrased in terms of 'if this happens then you do this, or else you do that'.

I also started to have staff training each other up in their respective roles. This was a real breakthrough because before I instituted this change, a staff member's tasks just didn't get done when they were away. It also meant that there could be times when one employee was snowed under while another was filling in time twiddling their thumbs until lunchtime came.

Sharing more tasks, learning each other's roles, and creating seamless workflows brought us to the point where we resembled the efficiency of McDonalds. Our future proof engine room was starting to run a lot more smoothly. I was building trust with employees and getting more confident when it came to delegating. This was something I was petrified about in the early years of my business because of the monkey on my back that believed no-one could do 'it' as well as me.

I started out on this path simply to find more time to work on the business. However, the benefits I accrued were far greater than I anticipated. For example, my staff started having a lot more confidence in their roles. What that meant was that when problems occurred, they had options other than asking me what to do. They had reference documents to go back to, and there were other team members who could jump in and assist them when they were busy.

It was great to see the team working more fluidly together. The result was that the culture started to blossom because there was a lot more interaction between team members, and they took a genuine interest in each other's roles because they had an insight into what each role entailed.

Thinking about this part of my business journey reminded me of a sort of possessiveness some of my staff displayed when the idea of sharing their expertise with their colleagues was suggested. The idea was aimed at stopping them from having to put in extra time as a result of increasing workloads. This was a time when my emotional intelligence came into its own, because all it took was a bit of reassurance about no one's job being at risk for everyone to get onboard. If anything, the strategy of sharing knowledge was about enriching everyone's roles while maintaining their wellbeing.

A bonus for me personally was that there was also an incredible journey of self-growth and self-discovery I went through during this period. Among other things, I realised that if I sensed a resistance in myself when it came to delegating certain tasks, it was an opportunity to reflect on whether the resistance was a result of my own insecurity and lack of strategic thinking. While this was going on, I started finding more time to work ON the business like a leader would, rather than being stuck IN the business like an operator.

When I first started doing less of the operational work, I was heartened to find that the business was still making the same profit (if not more) than it was when I was stuck in the weeds, so to speak. What's more, I was able to transition from working 60 hours per week to 50. I was still working consistently, but I was doing tasks that my unique skills were both needed for and ideally suited to. Of course, there were always going to be tasks that only I could do. That suited me just fine because I was able to be more focused on those tasks and lean into the business of effectively managing my business as well.

What's more, I really started to enjoy managing the business. This was a revelation because I hadn't ever experienced true management in any of the roles I held prior to starting my business. In law firms in particular, it always felt like everyone was doing their own thing. It was like there were ten mini businesses all under the same roof.

I was surprised when I found out how much I really enjoyed teaching and leading my team. I found the whole business of helping someone learn how to do something new to be a really fulfilling experience. With that new environment of collaboration and sharing in place within my business, I found myself creating real bonds with my team, and enjoying having regular and real connections with them. In turn, that enabled me to understand them better, and for them to understand me better as well.

Another really heartening result was that team members would come up with an idea around how to do something better than we were currently doing it from time to time. I smile whenever this happens because something like that would never have happened back in the days when I was working in old fashioned law firms. If anyone was ever brave enough to ask why something was done one way when they knew a better way to do it, they would hear words to the effect of "this is how we've always done it." Apparently, that was justification enough for not trying something new. Whereas I love nothing more than having staff members trying out a process with a fresh perspective that leads to a better way of doing something.

By this time the control freak in me had started to relax as the confidence within my team grew. That led to my confidence in them and in myself increasing as well, and the business becoming much more efficient. As a result, I started working less hours overall, and less hours as a technician versus the hours that I spent as a business owner.

In the first few years of my business where I was constantly in head down and bum up technician mode, I never had a moment to even think about the future of the business. It was a day by day, week by week scenario we had in place. However, the new changes I put in place allowed me to set long-term goals and strategies for growth. It also allowed time for things like networking, and leveraging social media to raise awareness of our services and my profile, as well as personal and professional development.

Finally, I was consciously and deliberately steering the direction of my business to achieve the goals I set. This resulted in greater profit for less effort. There was also the intangible benefit of the fact that I was doing more fulfilling tasks in an environment where I was learning and growing. I didn't notice it at the time, but in hindsight I could see that I'd become pretty stale spending hours and hours on mundane tasks before *The E-Myth* helped me to see the light. That changed everything. I even got to have my first holiday in six years!

The fact that (among other things) I was able to have a holiday resulted from the efficiencies I'd achieved as well as having more control over the business whether I was there in person or not. It also came down to the confidence I had built in myself. One of the realisations that brought this home to me was that I'd become a leader who makes proactive business decisions rather than reactive decisions related to the way the property market was looking. Another factor was that I had redirected my focus from the nuts and bolts of the business, to taking a strategic perspective. That shift ultimately led to a lot of growth in myself and the business.

That said, I still spend time operating on the technical aspects of my business. In fact, it's approximately 20% of my time. I happily do this because I love the conveyancing industry. I can afford to operate that way because I took the trouble to make changes where they were needed. I also got good at not shying away from things I'd rather avoid, such as having tough conversations.

The Art of Having Tough Conversations:
We are often faced with the need to have tough conversations in business and in life for that matter. Before I unpick this topic, I want to flesh out what a tough conversation actually is. I guess this definition could differ slightly from person to person, but for me it involves taking up a sensitive, challenging, or potentially confronting topic with someone. These conversations are often addressing issues that are uncomfortable and/or difficult to discuss.

The thing is that as leaders and business owners we have to be prepared to go there. I say that because what's at stake are things like clarity, understanding, growth, and the opportunity for the positive resolution of arguments. For example, dealing with a debtor who has not paid your invoice, or advising a client of a price increase, or counselling an underperforming employee, are the kinds of things that are an integral part of the role of business owners. The bottom line is that ducking and weaving because we'd rather have a tooth pulled than face the discomfort of having a tough conversation is no way to run a business.

I'd actually wager that it's the avoidance of making hard decisions and having tough conversations that plays no small part in the appalling percentage of businesses that go under within five years. Of course, a similar kind of scenario also plays out in our personal life as well. Can you think of something you've been avoiding talking to your partner about? Maybe it's connected to your finances, the distribution of housework, or different attitudes around raising kids. What I want to say is that you wouldn't be alone if you don't like having tough conversations around these kinds of topics.

One thing I've found is that tackling something I need to have a tough conversation about sooner rather than later tends to always result in a better outcome. That said, timing can be important, but please don't wait for the perfect time. I say that because there is no such thing. So if you ever catch yourself procrastinating, don't beat yourself up about it, but remember what's at stake. Sure, it might not be a question of life or death, but there will be something at stake that you can use to motivate yourself to get the job of having a tough conversation done and dusted.

When I opened my business, I was totally unprepared in relation to the fact that having tough conversations comes with the territory. I was a great conveyancer, which was all well and good, but there was nowhere for me to run and nowhere to hide because the inevitability of having to deal with a situation that entails a tough conversation was bound to come up sooner or later.

I don't know if you've ever heard anyone say that running a business is one of the best personal development journeys you could ever go on. For me, having to come to terms with reality and develop my skills around having tough conversations is a case in point. The thing is that most people (including me) are naturally conflict averse. So in a sense, we are wired to put off or completely avoid confronting someone and having a conversation they're not going to like. Instead of getting out of our comfort zone, we might resort to telling ourselves the problem will just resolve itself – in our dreams!

For example, I have an employee I'm going to call 'Diane' (that is not her real name). She has been on our team for 12 months when her performance started to drop. Her attention to detail and manner on phone calls was rapidly deteriorating. She was also becoming distant from the team, as well as not taking proper direction in meetings. Understandably the team was getting frustrated. It was time (or possibly past time if I'm honest) for me to step in and have a tough conversation with Diane about her inaccuracy, unacceptable performance and the effect it was having on the team.

It's lucky that this situation came about when I was in my later business years and not my first. This meant I had more refined skills that enabled me to handle the need for a tough conversation more confidently and effectively.

In the early days, I would have started the conversation listing off the things that Dianne had done wrong, and finished it off with an official warning. In other words, it would have been a one-way conversation. Whereas the Peta with a little more emotional intelligence started the conversation by telling Dianne that she was usually great at her job, but that I had noticed a significant drop in the quality of her work. Then I asked whether there was something going on that I needed to know about. That was a really important question to ask because it turned out that Diane was losing her hearing. She was worried about telling anyone because her role involved answering the phone a lot.

So, it turned out that rather than lacking the kind of diligence we were used to, Diane was trying her best to stay on top of everything while she was struggling to hear what people were saying to her, especially on the phone. After having our conversation Diane made an appointment and was able to get some hearing aids fitted. Within two weeks, she was a different person. She went back to being the bubbly, self-confident, accurate and valuable member of the team that she used to be. I'm pleased to say that Diane is still a very important member of my team to this day.

Over the years I've had many opportunities to hone my skills in having tough conversations. There've been some that have ended well, and some that didn't. The thing is that there is an art to having a tough conversation, and like a muscle, you need to practice it.

A book I love in this space is called *Radical Candor* by Kim Scott. I've taken this quote directly from the text describing the book on the Amazon platform which says "Radical Candor is the sweet spot between managers who are obnoxiously aggressive on the one side and ruinously empathetic on the other. It is about providing guidance, which involves a mix of praise as well as criticism – delivered to create better results and help employees develop their skills and boundaries of success." It goes on to say that "Great bosses have strong relationships with their employees, and Scott has identified three simple principles for building better relationships with your employees. They are to make it personal, get stuff done, and understand why it matters."

From where I sit, the ability to have tough conversations is important because it's central to our capacity to have solid authentic relationships with the people in our life, including our employees.

The dot points below represent the components Scott breaks down the challenge of planning for tough conversations into. I've included this here to help you develop your skills in this critical competency that can literally mean the difference between success and failure. The components in question are:

- Naming the issue
- Selecting a specific example that illustrates the behavior or situation you want to change
- Describing your emotions about this issue
- Clarifying what's at stake
- Identifying your contribution to the situation
- Indicating your wish to resolve the situation.

What I say when I'm mentoring my clients is that only good things come from having a difficult conversation. What's more, I remind them that whether it involves underperforming staff, disgruntled clients, unreliable business suppliers, bank managers, or whatever, the best way to have a difficult conversation is to just have it. And the sooner the better. The longer you leave it, the more angst you'll build up stewing over the awkwardness or worrying about what the outcome of the conversation is likely to be. Or worse, you'll avoid having the conversation altogether.

The problem with this approach is that it can lead to things like poor staff culture, frustrated clients, and terrible business relationships. Let alone the extra stress we generate when we stew over the topic.

I've had staff confess that they were worried about the possibility of generating a negative outcome from having a difficult conversation. What I say in reply, is that if the conversation is going to generate a negative outcome of some kind, they need to balance that with the real and present negative outcome the tough conversation is addressing. The other thing to add into the mix is that there's every chance the outcome they're expecting to come out of the tough conversation is still going to happen whether they have the conversation now or sometime later. What's more if they wait, they'll have to endure an extended period of stress. What this does is compound the negative effect of not having the tough conversation. Meanwhile, chances are there's a positive result waiting in the wings for the conversation to happen. That said, either way, it's better to get forward momentum, rather than putting yourself on edge for however long you put off having the conversation.

That's why I often say that only good things come from having a difficult conversation.

YOUR REFLECTIONS

- What are your strengths as a leader?
- How could you be a better leader?
- What can you do to delegate more effectively?
- How do you cultivate an environment where your team can thrive?
- Consider a tough conversation you've been avoiding. What steps can you take to prepare yourself to have the conversation constructively?

PART THREE:
World

CHAPTER SEVEN:
The Magic of Service

People will remember how you made them feel.

Providing high quality customer service is the bedrock of my business. We actually treat the saying you read above like a kind of pledge. Our whole approach to the customer experience is built around it. What we're all about is focusing on the feeling the client has when they turn up. With that in mind, we structure the way we provide our services with the view to having them leave feeling better than they did when they arrived.

Back in the day, I used to be hyper aware of my shortcomings (in my own head) when I didn't consider myself to be an expert in relation to a question a client might ask me. In fact, that was the kind of thing that used to activate my fear trigger to the extent that it would stop me from taking new things on. When I shifted my mindset to focus on how I could make my client feel better than they felt when they walked in, rather than the words I could say to impress them with my intelligence, our market share increased significantly.

In 2009 when I opened my conveyancing business I was only licensed to operate in NSW. It wasn't until 2021 that I had enough courage to obtain a conveyancing license in Victoria so that I could practice in both states. The longer I left getting qualified in Victoria, the bigger the gap around my knowledge of the law in the two states became. By the time I made the decision to open my business up to the Victorian market, I was an established expert in conveyancing in NSW and somewhat of a novice in Victoria.

Rather than focusing on the things I didn't know though, I focused on the strengths I had. That included a solid track record of, and natural ability to, take clients through their conveyancing journey so that they felt safe, secure, heard, and totally supported.

Fortunately, I was able to leverage my reputation for providing excellent service to launch into Victoria at top dollar. My reputation was such that even though I was more expensive than my competitors, as well as being new to the Victorian market, my business levels went up by 17% straight away. I believe this result was testament to the fact that people are prepared to pay extra for the experience they have when they sign up to work with myself and my team.

When I mentor upcoming conveyancers through their university years, I stress the importance of taking a nurturing approach when working with clients in the sometimes highly emotional space of buying or selling property. Some of them are surprised and grateful to find out that the way the client will feel when they sense we have their wellbeing at heart is a lot more important than dazzling them with facts about the complexities of the work we do. In other words, we don't have to know absolutely everything, and we certainly don't need to share everything we know with our clients. What's more, we can research anything we don't know off the top of our head, and let the client know that we will get back to them on any questions we can't answer on the spot.

So you might be wondering what it takes to achieve the kind of 5-star level of customer service required to create sustainable relationships like we do. The short answer is that it involves focusing on what I call the 1% things. In other words, it's things like customisation, attention to detail, and personalisation that will make all the difference. Anyone can be kind and courteous, but 5-star customer service is about going the extra mile. So I want you to think about what you can do to make your customers and/or clients feel special.

The good news is that it can be as simple as remembering their dog's name, or noticing the kind of tea they like when they come in for a meeting, or if they're someone who loves a chat vs those who like to get straight down to business. That way you can tailor the interactions you have with them to match their preferences.

Another way to think about maximising the experience your clients (and potential clients) have is to make sure you turn up to every interaction with a givers' mindset, not a takers' mindset. The concepts of givers' and takers' mindsets comes from the field of organisational psychology. You'll find an in-depth treatment of the topic in Adam Grant's book called *Give and Take*. While the context of the book is focussed on professional success, the idea of these mindsets can just as easily apply to the business of customer service. Here's how these two mindsets can play out in a customer service environment.

The Givers' Mindset:
In the context of customer service, having a givers' mindset is manifested in the following ways:

1. **Focussing on helping:** Givers prioritise the needs of the customer above all else. They genuinely want to help and solve problems for their customer, even if it requires going the extra mile.
2. **Valuing long-term relationships:** Givers are focussed on building lasting relationships with customers. They believe in creating positive, lasting impressions instead of only focusing on the immediate transaction.
3. **Demonstrating generosity in relation to information and resources:** A giver will willingly share information, provide additional resources, or take extra time to ensure the customer understands the solution they are proposing.
4. **Exuding empathy:** Givers tend to be more empathetic than takers. They try to understand the customer's perspective, and follow through with tailored assistance.

5. **Taking a collaborative approach:** Givers often work collaboratively with their customers and their colleagues to find the best solutions for the problem they're dealing with.

The Takers' Mindset:
On the other hand, a takers' mindset is characterised by:

1. **Acting from self-interest:** Takers are inclined to prioritise their own interests over the customer's. They might be more concerned about metrics, sales, or upselling than genuinely addressing the customer's needs.
2. **Focusing on short-term gains:** Takers are often more focused on the immediate transaction rather than the long-term relationship. They might be more likely to use aggressive sales tactics or prioritising a quick resolution over a thorough one tailored to the needs of the customer.
3. **Withholding information:** A taker might be inclined to not share information if they believe it serves their interest without regard to the right their client has to fulsome answers to their questions.
4. **Lacking genuine empathy:** While takers might feign concern, to achieve their immediate goal they're less likely to genuinely empathise with a customer's situation or feelings than those with a giver's mindset.
5. **Taking a competitive approach:** Takers are inclined to see customer interactions as a zero-sum game where in order to win, the other party (like the customer and/or their competitor) has to lose.

In the realm of customer service, a givers' mindset is more likely to foster trust, build brand loyalty, and ensure customer satisfaction. That said, it's important to strike a workable balance so that you and your employees don't burn out or feel as if you're being taken advantage of. On the other hand, while a takers' mindset might lead to short-term gains, it could harm an organisation's reputation and customer relationships in the long run.

From where I sit, whether you operate in a really competitive market or not, doing whatever you need to do to provide great customer service just makes sense. Your customers will be better off and so will you via the satisfaction that comes with a grateful client or customer. So, it just makes good sense to prioritise the quality of the customer service you provide.

On a side note, before we launch into the next chapter, I want to acknowledge the paradox relating to the fact that arguably one of the most important chapters in this book (i.e. this one) is by far the shortest. I guess that's because the importance of customer service is simply a given when it comes to business.

YOUR REFLECTIONS

- What does your business do to provide exceptional customer service?
- How do you tailor your customer interactions to make each client feel special and heard?
- Think about a situation where adopting a givers' mindset led to a positive outcome. What was the impact on the customer relationship?
- In what ways do you encourage your team to prioritise customer needs and build lasting relationships?
- What can you do to improve the level of customer service you provide?

CHAPTER EIGHT:
The Art of Social Media

Authenticity is your brand's best outfit.

What I want to say up front is that social media can be a blessing and a curse when it comes to people like us who are running a business. I say that because I'm pretty sure I'm not the only person who's opened up Facebook with the view to posting business content, only to find myself going down a rabbit hole. While being down the rabbit hole looking at someone's child taking their first step, or a puppy doing something cute can be heartwarming, it can also chew up valuable time that could be used more effectively.

Meanwhile, in my own case I've managed to build a strong profile on social media using the magic of a giver's mindset to enhance my standing and grow my business. The thing is that a well curated social media presence can open up a number of opportunities. These include networking opportunities, collaborations, speaking gigs, and potential customers. That's why it's so important to infuse our content with a generosity of spirit while demonstrating a level of expertise that makes us stand out.

The first step in using social media to build our business is to focus on the platforms that align with our goals. LinkedIn is a must for professional networking, while platforms like Instagram and Facebook can also be valuable depending on what industry we're in. Then it's a question of making sure our profile both reflects who we are, and makes a great first impression. This includes having a professional looking profile picture, a compelling bio, and a cover photo that reflects our brand.

We can also use keywords relevant to our area of expertise in our bio to improve visibility so that we show up in searches. I guess it goes without saying, but it's important to make sure our contact information is up to date and that it's actually there. You wouldn't be the first person if your ears pricked up when you read that sentence. Don't worry if you feel like you need to jump onto LinkedIn (or whatever platform/s you're using) right now and add your website and email address to your profile. The platforms have made this easy enough to do.

The question of what we post is where things get really interesting. I say that because our social media feed needs to reflect everything from our ethics, our knowledge, and our personality. What this looks like is sharing content that adds value to your followers. This includes things like industry insights, professional tips, and thought leadership articles. Original content in the form of blog posts or case studies that highlight current trends can also work really well to establish our expertise.

When I first opened my business, I slipped into taking a fairly 'standard' corporate approach to using social media. That resulted in the same kind of bland offering that seems to be the norm in the professional services space in particular. This space is full of polished posts with carefully drafted wording aimed at evoking a sense of trust, which is of course very important.

Whilst I appreciate the value of consistent branding in relation to building trust, it came to a point when I realised the standard approach wasn't setting me apart from anyone, including my competition. So, I got curious about how I could reach even more people and build trust while showing more of myself as the person behind the brand, so to speak.

What I discovered through trial and error was that engagement with my posts increased when I started approaching the business of social media with a giver's mindset. You'll remember I talked about the difference between a taker's and a giver's mindset in chapter seven. Just to remind you, what I mean by a giver's mindset is that the intention behind everything we do is to leave our audience feeling like we understand what they want. Further to that, it's about demonstrating that we're in the position to be able to consistently educate them with relevant content that in some way gets them closer to where they want to be.

This approach is all about providing information, knowledge, hints, and any number of other things that can help our audience without the dreaded 'call to action' that so many businesspeople finish their social media posts with. In my own case, I get a lot of engagement with posts like "Five things to look for during a pre-purchase inspection"; "Ten tips on choosing the right real estate agent"; and "How to prepare your home for an open house". This is in stark contrast to the sort of posts that result from a takers mindset that feel more like a little kid who's saying, "look at meeeeeeee".

Things really ramped up when I started doing a live video each Wednesday night on my social media channels. I did this at the same time each week, without fail. I saw it as an easy way to build trust, because among other things, people were in no doubt that I do what I say I will. In fact, it became so much fun that I would even do it when I was on holidays. I even did it when I was in Fiji and had to factor in time differences.

During these live videos I used to answer any questions my followers would ask. For the most part, people turned up with conveyancing and property related questions. They really appreciated the fact that I was essentially giving them free advice. These were really successful interactive sessions that enabled me to reach a different and wider audience. There was a lovely boomerang effect that took place because I was giving out advice and helping people which resulted in my attracting a whole new client base into my business.

People who signed up for my services would tell me that they felt as if they knew me because they'd seen me online. Basically, the interactive approach I took proved to be much more effective than even the most amazing images others were posting. It was like potential clients got to take me for a test ride. It was a bit of a 'try before you buy' scenario really.

A helpful bi-product of this strategy was that if someone didn't like my bold approach on social media, they wouldn't take the next step of contacting me with the view to engaging my services. The beauty of that is that enabling people who see my posts to get a feel for what I'm all about just brings the inevitable outcome forward. By that I mean that it saves both the potential client and me (or my staff) the time and effort of having to meet with the person to find out that we're not a match.

I found that the more vulnerable and genuine I was on social media, the more followers and engagement I got. I was even brought in to teach my approach at a lunch and learn session for the local chamber of commerce after they noticed what I was doing.

One of the questions I've been asked more than once is "aren't you scared your competitors will see what you're doing and copy you?" The answer is that I am not worried about that because if my competitors copy me, they will always be one step behind me. What's more, people are not stupid, they can see right through that type of behavior.

I'm actually used to having competitors copy me. And in the early years it did make me mad. That was before I learnt to trust my audience and remember that they could see that behavior for what it is. This all went on well before Tik Tok hit the scene and the power of social media went to the next level. So, I'd like you to reflect on what you could do now if you applied the recipe for building trust via social media that I created back in the day.

The situation now is that we have a much larger team, and I am not the sole conveyancer anymore, so our approach to social media has changed to reflect our current circumstances. The approach we use now is about putting the team in the picture as well. We make a point of highlighting the strengths of the team members so that clients won't feel like there're being short changed because I'm not the one dealing with them.

To this day, my personal social media presence is an extension of my business. By that I mean that I often share behind the scenes snapshots of my life. That includes everything from the high-performance habits I have ingrained into my days, to the way I run my business, to my focus on culture, and everything in between. As a result of this, I find that people make a decision to work with us because they agree with the way I do business, or they appreciate the way I treat my staff, and that kind of thing.

It's interesting to note that for the most part their decisions are not based on me being a great conveyancer. It's the fact that they feel like they can trust me that makes the difference. This confirms the saying that 'people buy people'. Further to that, it's because potential clients get an opportunity to feel like they know me and my team that opens the door to them trusting us.

At this point I feel like it's worth noting some of the unexpected advantages I've garnered by showing up on my social media channels with a giver's approach. They include:

- **Being offered speaking engagements**. People have approached me to deliver keynote talks, or write blog posts for their magazines and websites after discovering me online.
- **Attracting a high caliber of applicants when I need to recruit new staff**. The great majority of employment

opportunities in my business are filled from responses to social media posts I create about positions I have available. That means I rarely need to advertise externally. I simply create a social media post and the people who resonate with what I've written tend to be great applicants.

- **Making new connections**. As many of us don't have as much time to get out and about in the age of being super busy, I know I'm not the only one who's formed some amazing connections with people online. I know in my own case, that some of these contacts have turned into friends and close business colleagues. I know that a lot of businesspeople are scared of exposing themselves, or have some other kind of barrier when it comes to embracing social media. This is a real shame because it's not just a case of not taking advantage of the valuable exposure social media opens up to us, it's actually about the fact a lack of presence on social media could backfire and create distrust. I say that because it's not too much of a stretch to imagine people wondering what the person or business in question has to hide if they're not on any of the social media platforms. The thing is that whether you choose it or not, you will have an online presence anyway. If you doubt that, just google your name and your business and see what comes up.

The bottom line is that no matter how well you've managed to avoid getting involved with social media, there will always be a digital footprint that relates to you. So what I say is why not control the narrative? Why not show up so the digital footprint and presence you are putting out into the world is one you want the world to see?

If you were to ask me what tips I could share about getting the kinds of results I've managed to broker, I'd say:

Engage generously: Being generous on social media means engaging with your community in a meaningful way. I'd suggest commenting on, sharing, and liking content posted by your peers and industry leaders. As well as offering genuine praise, constructive feedback, and support where appropriate. Participating in discussions and offering your expertise can help build your reputation as a knowledgeable and generous professional.

Network proactively: Don't be shy about reaching out to others in your field on social media channels like LinkedIn in particular. Following industry leaders, joining professional groups, and participating in conversations on LinkedIn is very worthwhile. As is attending virtual events or webinars, and engaging with participants on social media, rather than being a passive observer. What's more, personalising connection requests with a note about why you're interested in connecting can make a big difference to the rate at which you're able to expand your network.

Maintain a professional profile: Always maintain professionalism in your interactions and the content you post. Avoiding controversial topics and be respectful in discussions. Remember that your social media presence is a reflection of your professional persona, and everything you share is public.

Regularly update your details: As your career or business develops, ensure your social media profiles are updated to reflect your current role, skills, and accomplishments. Regular updates keep your profile relevant and demonstrate that you are active and engaged in your professional development.

Monitor your digital footprint: Regularly review your social media profiles and search for your name online to see what comes up. This can help you to understand how others perceive your professional brand and allow you to make adjustments as needed.

The bottom line is that building a professional and generous profile on social media takes time and effort, but the rewards are well worth the trouble.

YOUR REFLECTIONS

- How do you feel about your presence on social media at the moment?
- Are you positioning yourself in a way that will attract people into your business?
- Are you posting content from the point of view of a giver's or a taker's mindset?
- Are you showing up on social media, or allowing the internet to create your digital footprint without you having a say?
- How could you be more genuine and show some of your real self in your social media posts?

CHAPTER NINE:
The Beauty of Competition

Learn from everyone, copy no one.

I'm going to share an anecdote with you to put my take on competition in context. It involves an occasion when I was carrying out negotiations on a client's behalf, and the way I handled myself in the negotiation was exemplary, if I say so myself. This was the exact opposite of the way the representative of the other party in the negotiation (who happened to be a competitor of mine) was behaving. It was a real lightbulb moment in terms of my understanding of what really matters to me. It also renewed my confidence about staying in my own lane. In other words, it was a great reminder to do what I do best without worrying about what others are doing.

You'll remember in an earlier chapter I talked about the way some of my competitors acted when I incorporated the word 'mentor' into my title. What I want to say in the event of something similar happening to you, is that when competitors attack you, or copy you, or try to damage your reputation in one way or other, it's actually a compliment. What's more, the fact they are bothering to do that is tantamount to being an advertisement about how good you actually are.

The thing to remember is that your audience is not silly, and they can see right through those who are jealous of your success. In other words, when you are excellent at what you do, your competitors who try to pull you down a peg or two will just look second rate to others. So please don't be tempted to get caught up in the drama of any foul play and the noise that comes with it. Use your energy to be exemplary at your craft and the service you provide, and you'll come out ahead every time.

My client Brett once emailed me these exact words: "Your competition is your greatest advertisement." It's something I've reminded myself of many times since I received this feedback. I'd love for him to be reading this book because he deserves to know that his words have rung in my ears many times when I needed to hear them. What's more, I have used them countless times with businesspeople I mentor. All I can say is "Thank you Brett from the bottom of my heart."

So my advice to you is to be grateful for the competition. This can be a tough pill to swallow sometimes. We open a new store, and another one similar opens up nearby. We come up with a brilliant idea, and someone else comes up with something similar shortly after we go public with it. Or maybe we publicly celebrate a milestone, and our competitor follows suit, or we lose a client or customer to a competitor. It's not uncommon for these kinds of things to happen. It's also not uncommon to resort to a bit of grumbling and wishing that competition didn't exist. Maybe you've even caught yourself fantasizing about how much bigger and better your business would be without that darn copycat down the road.

What I want you to do is experience how it feels to think about this topic differently. What thinking about it differently looks like is being grateful to your competition because if they weren't there, there's a risk you could become complacent. Maybe you wouldn't push yourself to excel as much as you do. Or maybe you wouldn't be as attuned to your customer's needs as you currently are. Perhaps you wouldn't even bother being customer centric at all, let alone bothering to find the defining uniqueness of your business that brings customers to your particular business rather than going to your competitors.

So next time your competitor's special announcement on social media has you in a hot sweat cursing "crap, why didn't I think of that first", I want you to stop and be grateful. It's moments like these that drive you to stay focused, and do what you do in your business better. That's why I say that blinkers aren't necessarily a bad thing. Sure, I know there are many books written by very successful entrepreneurs who will tell you it's good to know what your competitors are up to. But for me, this just doesn't ring true.

When I was spending time following my competitors and worrying about what they might be doing better than me, I was limiting myself creatively to their fields of vision. I say that because I was looking at what they were doing and determining what I would do on the basis of that. Instead, I found I had limitless potential when I stopped following their journeys and worrying about their progress.

Under those circumstances, my focus was on what I could do better than I currently was, not what I could do better than them. I also found some peace of mind in staying in my own lane with blinkers on so that I could really focus on my own business. The beauty of that was that it meant I wasn't ever going down rabbit holes wasting time reading reviews on the Google pages of my competitors, critiquing their web pages, or worrying about who was 'liking' their posts.

The bottom line is that once I started putting my metaphorical blinkers on and blocking out the white noise around what my competitors were doing, I was totally free to focus on charting my own path ahead. The beautiful thing was that all of a sudden life became a much simpler, more peaceful and distraction-free space for me to work in and thrive.

I want to encourage you to take this onboard because in the realm of business, competition is an inevitable, and in some cases even beneficial aspect of the dynamic at play. So I want to break down what adopting a healthy attitude towards competition looks like. Essentially it involves several key perspectives and attitudinal approaches including:

Viewing competition as a catalyst for innovation: Rather than perceiving competition as a threat, it's more productive to see it as a motivator for innovation and improvement. When businesses compete, they are pushed to enhance their products, services, and operational efficiencies. This drive for excellence not only benefits the business by fostering a culture of continual improvement, but also greatly benefits the consumers who receive better products and services because of it.

Focusing on your unique value proposition: In a competitive landscape, it's crucial to focus on what makes your business unique. This involves understanding your strengths and leveraging them in a way that differentiates you from your competitors. By concentrating on your unique value proposition, you can create a niche for your business that may be less vulnerable to competition.

Promoting healthy competition: Approaching competition with a spirit of fairness and ethical practices is vital. Healthy competition respects the rules of the industry and avoids underhanded tactics. Adopting this attitude not only enhances the reputation of your business, but also contributes to a more positive environment in the industry.

Being open to opportunities around collaboration: Sometimes competition can open doors for collaboration. Businesses can find ways to work together, like forming strategic alliances or partnerships that are mutually beneficial. This can be particularly effective in areas where companies complement, rather than directly compete with each other.

Maintaining a customer-centric approach: Ultimately, competition drives businesses to focus more on the customer. Understanding and meeting customer needs better than your competitors is a sure way to gain an edge in the market. This involves actively listening to customer feedback, and continuously adapting your offer to their evolving needs.

In conclusion, I want to say that the best attitude to adopt around the question of competition is what I call a realistically positive one. That entails not worrying about what's going on in your competitors' businesses, but letting the knowledge that they are there to motivate and strengthen your relentless drive for excellence, and an unwavering focus on customer satisfaction.

YOUR REFLECTIONS

- Can you recall a time when competition directly led to an improvement in your business?
- How do you distinguish your business's unique value in a competitive market?
- Have you considered opportunities for collaboration with competitors? What might that look like?
- In what ways has focusing on your customers helped you stand out against competition?
- Are you playing your own game or spending too much time and energy worrying about what your competition is doing?

CONCLUSION

I want to congratulate you for going the distance and making your way to the end of this book.

Running a successful business can be one of the most rewarding things to do. But it would be disingenuous to give you the impression that it will be a walk in the park if you play your cards right.

That said, running a business offers a multitude of rewards that can be both tangible and intangible, enriching the personal and professional lives of entrepreneurs. One of the obvious tangible rewards is the potential for financial gain. Unlike being employed, where earnings are typically fixed and capped by a salary or hourly wage, business ownership opens the door to unlimited income potential based on our company's success. This opportunity to directly reap the financial benefits of our hard work and innovation can be incredibly motivating and rewarding.

Beyond financial rewards, running a business also offers a sense of autonomy and freedom that is difficult to find in other career paths. Entrepreneurs have the liberty to make their own decisions, from setting their work schedules, to choosing who they work with, and what projects they take on. This level of control can lead to a more balanced and fulfilling life, where work aligns with personal values and goals.

Additionally, the challenge of building and growing a business can be immensely satisfying, providing a sense of achievement and personal growth. Entrepreneurs often take pride in creating something from nothing, overcoming obstacles, and making a positive impact on their community. My sense is that as you've made it to the end of this book, you might be somewhere on that journey.

If you'd like to know about my coaching, mentoring and conveyancing services, you can visit my website at www.petastewart.com.au

ABOUT THE AUTHOR

Peta Stewart is a conveyancing expert, entrepreneur, speaker and business mentor based in Albury NSW. Originally from Sydney, Peta relocated to Albury at the young age of five and has been a proud local ever since. In 2009, she founded her own conveyancing business, utilising her profound expertise to assist clients in navigating complex property transactions with ease.

Peta is also a former Australian Masters Track Cycling Champion and record holder. She harnesses the discipline and dedication from her high-performance sports background to drive high performance in business. Her approach to business mentoring incorporates dynamic skills that are applicable across various industries, making her guidance valuable to a diverse range of business professionals.

Her debut book draws from her extensive experience in both sports and business, offering invaluable insights into achieving success. It is a practical guide born from a desire to share the lessons she has learned and the mistakes she has made, aiming to help others thrive in their entrepreneurial endeavours.

Outside of her professional life, Peta is a devoted wife and stepmother, living in Albury with her husband, Daryl, and two stepchildren, Lucas and Riley. She is also a passionate dog lover, sharing her home with her beloved dogs, Gizmo, Billy, and Luna. Peta's commitment to her community and her passion for small business development in regional Australia are at the heart of her writing and mentoring efforts.

www.ingramcontent.com/pod-product-compliance
Lightning Source LLC
Chambersburg PA
CBHW061738070526
44585CB00024B/2727